GOD
CALLS YOU
Blessed,
GIRL

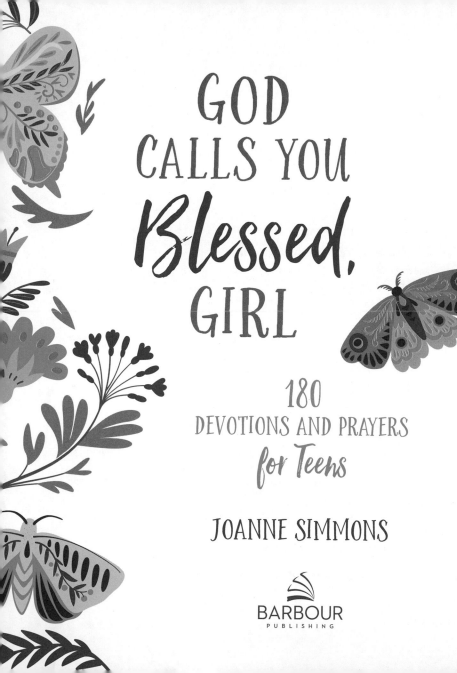

GOD
CALLS YOU
Blessed,
GIRL

180
DEVOTIONS AND PRAYERS
for Teens

JOANNE SIMMONS

BARBOUR
PUBLISHING

Member of the
Evangelical Christian
Publishers Association

INTRODUCTION

Do you ever stop to think about how incredible you are? Not in a full-of-yourself, arrogant kind of way but in a matter-of-fact, awestruck kind of way. Every cell in your body has been put together in the most amazing living, breathing, interworking system. You see, and you feel, and you hear. You taste and smell. You think, and you learn, and you acquire new skills. You move and produce and create and design—all of your own free will. But you are not just some temporary machine. Your body holds your soul, which has been created to last forever. This is all by design of the Master Designer, the one true Creator God. He knit you together in your mother's womb and created you with specific plans and a purpose.

So you surely are blessed, girl! That means you're fortunate, happy, and especially favored! God created humans in His image—as His very best part of creation. When we seek to know our Creator and His perfect plans for us more and more each day, we can't help but be full of deep gratitude for just how wonderfully blessed we are.

THE BEST KIND OF BLESSED

Those who belong to Christ will not suffer the punishment of sin.
ROMANS 8:1 NLV

The best way your heavenly Father wants you to know you are blessed is by giving you salvation and eternal life. That is the most important message you can ever hear. And what you do with that message is the most important decision you'll ever make. Do you know the gospel message? Here it is: Because the first two people God created, Adam and Eve, made a terrible decision to disobey God, sin has been messing with everyone everywhere ever since. And there's a big price to pay for sin—suffering and death in this world. But the good news of the gospel is that God loves us so much that He sent His Son, Jesus Christ, to show all people His glory and to be the one and only way, truth, and life for us. Jesus willingly gave up His life on the cross and died to pay for our sin. When we admit our sin and trust in Jesus Christ as our Savior, we are given the most amazing gifts of grace that covers our sin and new life that lasts forever. We begin our new life in Christ immediately as we allow Him to be our Lord and choose to follow and obey Him.

• •

Dear Jesus, I believe that You died on the cross to pay the price for my sin and then rose again, defeating death. Please forgive me and save me and give me eternal life. I want You alone to be Lord of my life. With Your help, I want to love and follow and obey You all of my days. Amen.

YOU ARE BLESSED
BY THE HOLY SPIRIT

[Jesus said,] "These things I have spoken to you while being present with you. But the Helper, the Holy Spirit, whom the Father will send in My name, He will teach you all things, and bring to your remembrance all things that I said to you. Peace I leave with you, My peace I give to you; not as the world gives do I give to you. Let not your heart be troubled, neither let it be afraid."

JOHN 14:25–27 NKJV

After Jesus lived and died and rose again and returned to heaven, God never intended to leave us alone in this crazy world. So not only do we have the blessings of grace that covers our sin and life that lasts forever, we also have the Holy Spirit. The Holy Spirit is our comforter, our counselor, and our guide. The Holy Spirit cares for us and even prays for us when we don't know what to pray (Romans 8:26). God knows everything we think and say and do, but that should never freak us out—His watchful gaze is something to be incredibly grateful for because He loves and cares for us like no one else.

. . . .

Heavenly Father, remind me that You are with me constantly through the presence of the Holy Spirit. I am never alone, never forgotten, never without help and hope. Help me to sense Your Holy Spirit in everything I do, and help me to listen and be guided well. Amen.

YOU ARE BLESSED BY THE BIBLE AND PRAYER

All Scripture is inspired by God and is useful to teach us what is true and to make us realize what is wrong in our lives. It corrects us when we are wrong and teaches us to do what is right. God uses it to prepare and equip his people to do every good work.

2 TIMOTHY 3:16–17 NLT

You know that when you begin a good relationship with someone, it takes effort or you won't stay in a good relationship. We can't just ignore or ghost someone and remain close. And we can't ignore or ghost God and expect to remain close to Him either. So how do we maintain a good relationship? First, we read and listen to and follow God's Word, the Bible. God has given us a living and active book (Hebrews 4:12) to communicate with us. When we read it with a humble, teachable attitude and also talk with God through prayer, asking Him to teach and guide us through it, we grow deeper in our knowledge of and love for our heavenly Father, closer in our walk with Jesus, and more aware of the Holy Spirit's presence and involvement in our lives.

Heavenly Father, thank You for the blessing of the Bible. Help me to love Your Word and learn it well so that I continually grow closer to You and Your will for my life—and further away from sin and evil. Amen.

YOU ARE BLESSED TO HEAR AND OBEY

[Jesus] replied, "Blessed rather are those who
hear the word of God and obey it."
LUKE 11:28 NIV

Maybe you sit in class without really paying attention sometimes. It happens to even the best of students. It's easy to hear but not really listen. And it's easy to hear and listen but not actually do anything with what we've heard and learned. God knows this is true of everyone, and His Word instructs us about people who hear the Word of God but don't do anything with it. James 1:22–25 (NIV) says, "Do not merely listen to the word, and so deceive yourselves. Do what it says. Anyone who listens to the word but does not do what it says is like someone who looks at his face in a mirror and, after looking at himself, goes away and immediately forgets what he looks like. But whoever looks intently into the perfect law that gives freedom, and continues in it—not forgetting what they have heard, but doing it—they will be blessed in what they do."

. . . .

Heavenly Father, please help me to obey Your Word
and live out what it says with a sincere heart and
mind, being truly happy to serve You! Amen.

YOU CAN CRAVE GOD'S WORD

I have hidden your word in my heart, that I might not sin against you. I praise you, O LORD; teach me your decrees. I have recited aloud all the regulations you have given us. I have rejoiced in your laws as much as in riches. I will study your commandments and reflect on your ways. I will delight in your decrees and not forget your word.
PSALM 119:11–16 NLT

We are so blessed when we can honestly say these words of Psalm 119 are true in our lives. But it sure can be hard to keep up good habits of reading and focusing our thoughts on God's Word, especially with all the other things going on in life. And we have a sin nature and an enemy that try to keep us from the good habit of spending time in God's Word. So we need to ask God to help us look forward to reading and studying the Bible every day. We need to ask Him to help us *crave* it.

· ·

Father God, I want to crave Your Word and a relationship with You more than anything else. But so many distractions try to pull me away from time with You. Please help me to be disciplined and wise! Amen.

YOU CAN TRUST GOD'S WORD

We also thank God constantly for this, that when you received the word of God, which you heard from us, you accepted it not as the word of men but as what it really is, the word of God, which is at work in you believers.

1 THESSALONIANS 2:13 ESV

Do you ever stop and wonder, or do some of your friends ever ask you, "How do I know the Bible is true? Why should I trust it?" If you take time to look, you will find amazing research from experts throughout history who verify why the Bible can be trusted far more than any other book ever written. Check out great resources like Answers in Genesis and author Josh McDowell for some good information. More importantly, constantly remember that you have a relationship with God Himself through Jesus Christ, and you have the Holy Spirit within you. As you read the Bible consistently over time, ask God to show you more about Himself through His Word. Ask Him to grow your faith, and then trust Him to do it! You will be amazed at how He answers your prayers.

. . . .

Heavenly Father, please keep growing my faith in You as I read Your awesome Word! Show me how and why it's true and can be trusted. Amen.

YOU CAN RUN FAR AWAY FROM SIN

Happy is the man who does not walk in the way sinful men tell him to, or stand in the path of sinners, or sit with those who laugh at the truth. . . . For the Lord knows the way of those who are right with Him. But the way of the sinful will be lost from God forever.

PSALM 1:1, 6 NLV

Especially in your teenage and young adult years, the world will tell you how fun it is to play around with sin and risky behavior. But the world lies. God's Word tells you to run away from the evil desires of youth and pursue righteousness, faith, love, and peace instead (2 Timothy 2:22). Watch even a few minutes of the daily news. Do you want to trust this crazy, broken world and dabble in sin, or do you want to trust the never-changing God who gives you life and your every breath and who loves You so much He even let His only Son die for you?

• •

Dear Lord, please help me to stand strong in my love for You, my faith in You, and my obedience to You, no matter what crazy thing the world is telling me is harmless and just for fun. Remind me of Your deep love and great sacrifice to pay for my sin so that I will never want to play around with evil. Amen.

13

YOU CAN MAKE PRAISE A PRIORITY

"Let the heavens be glad. Let the earth be filled with joy. And let them say among the nations, 'The Lord rules!' Let the sea thunder, and all that is in it. Let the field be happy, and all that is in it. Then the trees of the woods will sing for joy before the Lord. For He is coming to judge the earth. O give thanks to the Lord, for He is good. His loving-kindness lasts forever."

1 CHRONICLES 16:31–34 NLV

You are blessed when praising God is a priority in your life. Maybe you need to put down your phone more often to make time. Maybe you need to stop stressing over studying for a bit to make time. Maybe you need to tell your friends you need some time alone with God. Whatever you need to do, take time to be still before God (Psalm 46:10) regularly. Focus on His creation and tell Him how awesome He is and how grateful you are for His goodness.

* *

Almighty God, You are incredible! I am delighted and amazed by You—no one else is like You! I praise You, and I'm so grateful to be loved and known by You. Amen.

YOU ARE BLESSED BY DESIGN

So God created human beings in his own image. In the image of God he created them; male and female he created them. Then God blessed them and said, "Be fruitful and multiply. Fill the earth and govern it. Reign over the fish in the sea, the birds in the sky, and all the animals that scurry along the ground." . . . Then God looked over all he had made, and he saw that it was very good!

GENESIS 1:27–28, 31 NLT

We are blessed by God's good design for people in His creation. Various people and cultures and societies have made up all kinds of theories about how the world began and what the purpose and meaning of life is, but how can they all be true? If they are all true and everyone can make up their own truth, then nothing is actually true. There has to be one source of ultimate truth—and that source is the one true God. We find the truth behind the origins and design of this world in the book of Genesis, and God's whole Word in context continues the story that gives all life meaning and purpose.

• •

Heavenly Father, You alone are the one true God. You are Creator and You are Master Designer. I'm so blessed to believe in You and follow Your Word. I pray that more and more people will come to believe in You too! Amen.

YOU CAN TRUST IN THE LORD

"Blessed are those who trust in the Lord and have made the Lord their hope and confidence. They are like trees planted along a riverbank, with roots that reach deep into the water. Such trees are not bothered by the heat or worried by long months of drought. Their leaves stay green, and they never stop producing fruit."
JEREMIAH 17:7–8 NLT

Can you name a single person who has never let you down? Even if you can, it just means you don't know the person well enough or haven't known them long enough. No person on earth is perfect. Yes, God mercifully blesses us with trustworthy people; it's just that even the most reliable person on earth is never 100 percent reliable. They're always capable of disappointing or hurting us, intentionally or not, because they are human and have a sin nature. We need and are grateful for good people relationships, but we are most blessed when we look to God above all and put our full trust in Him, knowing our most important relationship is with Him. He alone is perfect and worthy of our praise.

. . . .

Lord, my relationship with You is the most important relationship in my life. You are love itself, and You are my real hope. I trust in You more than anyone else. You give me all the strength and confidence I need. Amen.

16

YOUR NEEDS ARE PROVIDED, PART 1

*God will supply every need of yours according
to his riches in glory in Christ Jesus.*
PHILIPPIANS 4:19 ESV

Maybe you're short on money right now. Maybe bills are due and there's no way to pay for them. Your family might be going through a hard time financially, or you need an after-school job and you just can't find one. Whatever the case, let this promise from God's Word give you reassurance and peace. Those who love God and follow Jesus will have all their needs met. Our heavenly Father knows exactly what we need before we even ask Him (Matthew 6:8). So don't fuss or fret. Keep being faithful and obedient to God and His Word and keep seeking His will, and then watch how He provides and blesses in amazing ways.

* *

Heavenly Father, I admit I'm worried right now about things I truly need that I'm not sure I'll be able to afford. Help me to trust in Your promises to provide. Please show me how to be faithful and obedient no matter my budget or bank account. You can provide in miraculous ways, and I'm believing You will. Amen.

YOUR NEEDS ARE PROVIDED, PART 2

Christ will make his home in your hearts as you trust in him. Your roots will grow down into God's love and keep you strong. And may you have the power to understand, as all God's people should, how wide, how long, how high, and how deep his love is. May you experience the love of Christ, though it is too great to understand fully. Then you will be made complete with all the fullness of life and power that comes from God. Now all glory to God, who is able, through his mighty power at work within us, to accomplish infinitely more than we might ask or think. Glory to him in the church and in Christ Jesus through all generations forever and ever!

EPHESIANS 3:17–21 NLT

If you're in the middle of a financial struggle, waiting and praying and wondering how God is going to provide, let this passage from Ephesians calm you down and comfort you. When you focus on how great God's love for you is and how He is able to do so much more than you could ever even dream up, peace will fill your heart and push away the anxiety as you wait for God's blessings.

· ·

Heavenly Father, please forgive me for worrying too much. I want to focus on the facts of how much You love me and how capable You are to provide above and beyond what I can even imagine. Thank You for knowing my needs and meeting them—and providing many extra blessings on top! Amen.

WORK WON'T WORK

People are counted as righteous, not because of their work, but because of their faith in God who forgives sinners. David also spoke of this when he described the happiness of those who are declared righteous without working for it: "Oh, what joy for those whose disobedience is forgiven, whose sins are put out of sight. Yes, what joy for those whose record the LORD has cleared of sin."

ROMANS 4:5–8 NLT

We are so greatly blessed that work won't save us from our sin and get us to heaven. Imagine how exhausting working for our salvation would be, how much anxiety we'd feel as we wondered if we were doing a good enough job! Thankfully, our salvation is a gift from God that we receive from Him because of our faith. We believe that God provided Jesus to pay the price for our sin, and we believe that Jesus died on the cross and rose again. We believe that the only way to be made right with God is through Jesus Christ. We admit our sin and ask God to forgive us for it, and we let Jesus be Lord over our lives, doing our best to obey Him and follow His ways, which we learn from the Bible and guidance of the Holy Spirit.

Father God, thank You that I could never work my way to heaven. You never expected me to. I could never pay the price for my sin on my own, so You gave Jesus as my Savior. I am beyond grateful, and I want to live all my life to honor and praise You. Amen.

YOU ARE BLESSED (OR NOT) THROUGH FRIENDSHIP

Walk with the wise and become wise; associate with fools and get in trouble. Trouble chases sinners, while blessings reward the righteous.
PROVERBS 13:20–21 NLT

Are you blessed through your friendships or not? Good friends who love and trust Jesus as Savior and who encourage us (1 Thessalonians 5:11) in our walk with Him are truly a blessing. But those who don't require extra caution. Of course we want to have friendships with nonbelievers and hopefully help lead them to salvation in Jesus at some point. But we never want them to lead us away from Jesus with a stronger influence on us than we have on them. God's Word is clear that "bad company corrupts good character" (1 Corinthians 15:33 NIV). As we enjoy friendship, we need to ask God to help us have relationships that are pleasing and honoring to Him.

. . . .

Dear Jesus, please bless me with good friends who love You like I do. Help me to be very careful with friends who don't walk with You as their Savior. I pray that I can help lead them to You, but I never want them to pull me away from You. Please give me wisdom and fun and joy and encouragement as I build relationships that bring glory to You. Amen.

YOU HAVE MARY'S EXAMPLE

Elizabeth gave a glad cry and exclaimed to Mary, "God has blessed you above all women, and your child is blessed. . . .When I heard your greeting, the baby in my womb jumped for joy. You are blessed because you believed that the Lord would do what he said."

LUKE 1:42–45 NLT

Mary was blessed "above all women" to be chosen by God to be the mother of Jesus, to carry and nurture the Savior of the world. And it wasn't going to be an easy task. Her song of praise and her obedience and joy give us an example of what our attitude should be when we are blessed to be chosen by God to do important work for Him, no matter the difficulty:

Mary responded, "Oh, how my soul praises the Lord. How my spirit rejoices in God my Savior! For he took notice of his lowly servant girl, and from now on all generations will call me blessed. For the Mighty One is holy, and he has done great things for me. He shows mercy from generation to generation to all who fear him. His mighty arm has done tremendous things! He has scattered the proud and haughty ones. He has brought down princes from their thrones and exalted the humble. He has filled the hungry with good things and sent the rich away with empty hands. He has helped his servant Israel and remembered to be merciful. For he made this promise to our ancestors, to Abraham and his children forever." (Luke 1:46–55 nlt)

· ·

Heavenly Father, help me to remember Mary's example and respond like she did to Your will for my life. Amen.

YOU CAN BE PATIENT AND PERSEVERE

*Be patient, then, brothers and sisters, until the Lord's coming.
See how the farmer waits for the land to yield its valuable crop,
patiently waiting for the autumn and spring rains. You too, be
patient and stand firm, because the Lord's coming is near. . . .
Brothers and sisters, as an example of patience in the face of
suffering, take the prophets who spoke in the name of the Lord.
As you know, we count as blessed those who have persevered. You
have heard of Job's perseverance and have seen what the Lord
finally brought about. The Lord is full of compassion and mercy.*

JAMES 5:7–11 NIV

It's understandable and common to grow weary and discouraged by
doing the right thing and believing and following the one true God and
His Word in a world that increasingly rejects Him. But as this scripture
reminds us, the Lord is full of compassion and mercy. He cares, and He
sees our faithfulness. We can look back to examples of those who persevered before us and were greatly blessed, like Job, and be encouraged to
keep on keeping on as we follow Jesus and wait for His return.

*Dear Jesus, sometimes I grow impatient and weary while I'm working
hard and waiting for You. But with Your help, I will continue to be
patient and persevere. I trust in You and Your blessings. Amen.*

22

WHEN YOU NEED A POWERFUL PEP TALK

*"Be strong and very courageous. Be careful to obey all the law my
servant Moses gave you; do not turn from it to the right or to the
left, that you may be successful wherever you go. Keep this Book
of the Law always on your lips; meditate on it day and night,
so that you may be careful to do everything written in it. Then you
will be prosperous and successful. Have I not commanded you?
Be strong and courageous. Do not be afraid; do not be discouraged,
for the LORD your God will be with you wherever you go."*

JOSHUA 1:7–9 NIV

God called Joshua to be the one who would lead His people into the
promised land after wandering in the desert for forty years. In Joshua
1, you can read the powerful pep talk God gave Joshua to help him be
the brave new leader. It's not just for Joshua though. You can read this
scripture and let God powerfully pep talk you as well, as He leads you
into the wonderful plans He has for your life!

• •

*Father God, thank You for Your powerful pep talk to Joshua
long ago. Thank You too that I can be strengthened and
encouraged by those same words even now. Amen.*

"BLESSED" ACCORDING TO JESUS

[Jesus said,] "Blessed are the poor in spirit, for theirs is the kingdom of heaven. Blessed are those who mourn, for they will be comforted. Blessed are the meek, for they will inherit the earth. Blessed are those who hunger and thirst for righteousness, for they will be filled. Blessed are the merciful, for they will be shown mercy. Blessed are the pure in heart, for they will see God. Blessed are the peacemakers, for they will be called children of God. Blessed are those who are persecuted because of righteousness, for theirs is the kingdom of heaven. Blessed are you when people insult you, persecute you and falsely say all kinds of evil against you because of me. Rejoice and be glad, because great is your reward in heaven, for in the same way they persecuted the prophets who were before you."

MATTHEW 5:3–12 NIV

Jesus' words in this well-known passage of the Bible called the Beatitudes sound so upside-down opposite from what the world tells us will make us happy and content. Contrary to the popular messages of our day, wealth and fame and status and power are not our real sources of blessing. Really, we are blessed when we are humble and do the will of God, loving Him above all and caring for others as He directs us to. In service to our heavenly Father is where we find true and lasting blessings both here on earth and for eternity.

. . . .

Dear Lord, I want the blessings that You say are best of all. Please help me to love You, love others, and do the good things You have created me to do. Amen.

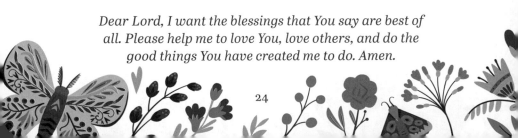

24

YOU CAN HOLD YOUR HEAD HIGH

The Lord will be your confidence.
PROVERBS 3:26 ESV

We've all done things that were embarrassing or awkward. You know, those things that made us want to melt into the floor or become invisible. And after these kinds of experiences, the weirdness can live on in our minds for a long time. But the awkward or embarrassing moment is usually much bigger in our own minds than in the minds of others. Yes, whoever was watching might remember for a while. You might even get teased a little. But that shows others' character, not yours. You can choose to show strong character and courage by remembering that everyone has embarrassing moments. So shake it off. Hold your head high, remembering you are a child of the one true God who loves you and is always looking out for you—no matter what embarrassing things you (and everyone else) might do.

. . . .

Heavenly Father, when I'm dealing with embarrassment, please comfort me and help me to shake it off. Help me remember that You are my confidence. Thank You for loving me no matter what. Amen.

YOU HAVE THIS FIRST COMMANDMENT WITH A PROMISE

Children, obey your parents because you belong to the Lord, for this is the right thing to do. "Honor your father and mother." This is the first commandment with a promise: If you honor your father and mother, "things will go well for you, and you will have a long life on the earth."

EPHESIANS 6:1–3 NLT

Especially as a teen, you might constantly hear the (dumb) idea that it's uncool to obey your parents. But what does the Bible say? And do you want to follow the crowd and their often destructive trends or follow God's Word and the eternal goodness He wants for you? Notice specifically verses 2 and 3 (NLT): "This is the first commandment with a promise: If you honor your father and mother, 'things will go well for you, and you will have a long life on the earth.'" Wow, it sounds like obeying your parents is kind of a big deal, right? Don't ever forget this commandment and promise from God. Do your best to honor and obey your mom and dad, and let God bless your entire life because of it.

. . . .

Dear Lord, thank You for the blessing of my parents in this world. I love them. It's not always easy to honor and obey them, because I often want to go my own way and do my own thing. But please help me to have joy in honoring and obeying my parents because I remember Your commands and Your promise of blessings. Amen.

YOU ARE WONDERFULLY MADE

You created my inmost being; you knit me together in my mother's womb. I praise you because I am fearfully and wonderfully made; your works are wonderful, I know that full well. My frame was not hidden from you when I was made in the secret place, when I was woven together in the depths of the earth. Your eyes saw my unformed body; all the days ordained for me were written in your book before one of them came to be. How precious to me are your thoughts, God! How vast is the sum of them!

PSALM 139:13–17 NIV

God made you and has known every detail about you since the moment you were first conceived. That truth should give you amazing confidence that you are deeply known and loved by the Creator of the universe. Call out to God in praise for the awesome way He has made you. Talk to Him constantly about the wonderful works He has done and the ones He wants to continue to do through you.

. . . .

Father God, I'm amazed at how You created me, how You know me and love me! I don't think I can fully understand Your love for me, but I never want to stop trying to know You better. Please guide me through every day You have ordained for me. Amen.

YOU HAVE NOAH'S EXAMPLE

Noah. . .did all that God commanded him.
GENESIS 6:22 ESV

Most people know at least a little about the story of Noah in the Bible, and it's good to read and remember it. God was pleased with Noah, and then He gave Noah some instructions that must have seemed totally crazy! Build a giant ark? Collect two of each animal and load them up along with the family? Then wait while the rains fall and completely flood and destroy the whole earth? Even though Noah was an exceptionally good man, he probably shook his head sometimes, wondering what on earth was going on. Still, he continued to obey God. And in the end, God did exactly what He said He would do: He destroyed every living thing with a great flood. Only Noah and his family and the animals they had gathered survived, safe inside the ark. Noah and his family were greatly blessed because of Noah's obedience. Have you ever sensed God leading you to do something that seemed to make zero sense, but you obeyed and then were blessed for it? Remember those times regularly, and thank and praise God for them!

. . . .

*Heavenly Father, please help me to learn from Noah's
example of obedience to You. Even when I don't understand,
I want to follow Your commands and direction. Amen.*

YOU ARE THE LIGHT OF THE WORLD

"You are the light of the world—like a city on a hilltop that cannot be hidden. No one lights a lamp and then puts it under a basket. Instead, a lamp is placed on a stand, where it gives light to everyone in the house. In the same way, let your good deeds shine out for all to see, so that everyone will praise your heavenly Father."
MATTHEW 5:14–16 NLT

What a beautiful thing to get up in the morning and tell yourself as you look in the mirror, "You are the light of the world." That's what Jesus has said of you and me when we trust Him as Savior. With the Holy Spirit living inside us, our job is to shine our lights so that others will want to trust Jesus as Savior and praise God too! We should never want to cover up our light. The dark world around us needs the good news and love of Jesus desperately, so we need to shine as brightly as possible!

* *

Dear Jesus, I am blessed to be the light of the world because of You! I want to shine Your love brightly to everyone around me and give God all the praise! Amen.

YOUR GOD IS HOLY

I saw the Lord sitting on a throne, high and honored. His long clothing spread out and filled the house of God. Seraphim stood above Him, each having six wings. With two he covered his face, and with two he covered his feet, and with two he flew. One called out to another and said, "Holy, holy, holy, is the Lord of All. The whole earth is full of His shining-greatness."
ISAIAH 6:1–3 NLV

In this scripture the prophet Isaiah is describing a vision he had of God, sitting on His throne with angels called seraphim surrounding Him and worshipping Him. To call God holy means to lift Him high above all others, esteeming Him as perfect and worthy of total devotion—meaning all your attention. No matter what is going on in your life, you'll be blessed if you take time each day to stop and think about God's holiness and praise Him for it. He is above all and absolutely perfect and awesome. And He loves you and cares about every detail of your life. That's an incredible blessing to be grateful for!

* *

Almighty God, You are holy, holy, holy! I'm in awe of You and so blessed by You. Amen.

YOU ARE THE BEAUTIFUL WORK OF GOD'S HAND

But now, O Lord, you are our Father; we are the clay,
and you are our potter; we are all the work of your hand.

ISAIAH 64:8 ESV

Do you remember drawing or painting something or sculpting something out of clay when you were little, and you knew exactly what it was meant to be, but no one else seemed to? That's because you were the creator, so of course you knew, even if no one else could see it. Never forget that the one true God is your Creator. Sometimes you might not be sure exactly who you are meant to be and what you're supposed to be doing as you're growing and still figuring life out, but God always knows. Keep following Him and asking Him to guide you into the extraordinary life He made you for, full of the good things He has planned for you.

• •

Dear God, You are the potter and I am the clay. Thank You for
making me and having good plans for me. Please show me day by
day what those plans are. I want to follow You forever! Amen.

YOU CAN CONFESS AND BE BLESSED

Come and listen, all you who fear God, and I will tell you what he did for me. For I cried out to him for help, praising him as I spoke. If I had not confessed the sin in my heart, the Lord would not have listened. But God did listen! He paid attention to my prayer.

PSALM 66:16–19 NLT

To have total confidence that God listens to and answers our prayers, we need to regularly admit our sins to God. The Bible is clear that God forgives us and removes our sin as far as the east is from the west (Psalm 103:12), but first we need to confess those sins to Him. That keeps us humble and depending on God, which is the best blessing, because no one is greater or more powerful than our good and loving heavenly Father.

* *

Dear God, You know I make many mistakes, and I don't want to hide them or pretend like I don't sin. These are my sins: _____. Please forgive me for them and remove them from me. Thank You that You do! Amen.

YOU HAVE SALVATION AND PURPOSE

God saved you by his grace when you believed. And you can't take credit for this; it is a gift from God. Salvation is not a reward for the good things we have done, so none of us can boast about it. For we are God's masterpiece. He has created us anew in Christ Jesus, so we can do the good things he planned for us long ago.

 EPHESIANS 2:8–10 NLT

You can probably think of friends and classmates who seem hopeless and without purpose. They don't seem to care much about anything. They don't seem to have goals or plans. Or maybe they do have goals and plans, but they're on the wrong track or they're doing good things but for the wrong reasons. Either of those can lead to depression or anxiety. But focusing on Ephesians 2:8–10 is the best motivation. When you think about how God gave you the gift of salvation and created you on purpose with good plans for your life, you should feel full of gratitude and enthusiasm, eager to keep seeking God and asking Him to guide you in doing all those good things He has ready and scheduled for you in His perfect timing.

* *

Heavenly Father, thank You for salvation and new life in Jesus Christ. Thank You for creating me with purpose and plans. I'm excited for You to show me all the good things You want me to do with my life. Day by day, I'll trust You and follow Your lead. Amen.

YOU CAN BE TOTALLY CONTENT

I have learned to be happy with whatever I have. I know how to get along with little and how to live when I have much. I have learned the secret of being happy at all times. If I am full of food and have all I need, I am happy. If I am hungry and need more, I am happy. I can do all things because Christ gives me the strength.

PHILIPPIANS 4:11–13 NLV

"Comparison is the thief of joy" is a well-known quote attributed to Theodore Roosevelt. And social media is often where the most comparison and joy-stealing goes on these days. The way to not let your joy be stolen is to be totally content the way God's Word says. Contentment means being happy and satisfied with what you have. It means you're not wanting something other than what you already have. God can give you total contentment when you focus on how you can do anything, get through any circumstance, with Jesus Christ giving you strength. Sometimes in life you might have more than enough, while other times you feel like you don't have nearly enough, especially when you look around too much in comparison. But when you focus on God and trust that He gives you exactly what you need when you need it, then you can be peaceful and thankful all the time.

• •

Dear Jesus, please help me remember how to be totally content—by trusting I can do all things because You make me strong to face anything! Amen.

WHEN YOU'RE TESTED AND TEMPTED

God blesses those who patiently endure testing and temptation. Afterward they will receive the crown of life that God has promised to those who love him. And remember, when you are being tempted, do not say, "God is tempting me." God is never tempted to do wrong, and he never tempts anyone else. Temptation comes from our own desires, which entice us and drag us away. These desires give birth to sinful actions. And when sin is allowed to grow, it gives birth to death.

JAMES 1:12–15 NLT

Anyone who thinks that becoming a Christian means enjoying an easy life is clearly not actually reading the Bible or growing closer to God. His Word plainly says that we will be tested and tempted to do wrong. Even so, loving God and trusting in and following Jesus as Lord and Savior make for the best kind of life. In every test and temptation, every bit of suffering and heartache, God is working out His good plans in our lives when we faithfully obey Him no matter our circumstances. He blesses us with His supernatural comfort and peace and joy even in the midst of the trials and pain, until one day we will have total comfort, peace, and joy—and no tears or hardship ever again—when we are at home forever in heaven.

Heavenly Father, please help me to patiently endure the tests and temptations in my life. I want to prevail over them as I follow You and keep my faith in Your eternal blessings.

YOU HAVE DEBORAH'S EXAMPLE

Deborah, a woman who spoke for God, was judging Israel at that time. She would sit under the tree of Deborah between Ramah and Bethel in the hill country of Ephraim. And the people of Israel came to her to find out what was right or wrong.

JUDGES 4:4–5 NLV

Deborah was the only woman to serve as a judge of the nation of Israel. So cool! God used her to free His people from the control of evil King Jabin of Canaan. She sent for a man named Barak and told him the instructions God had given to defeat King Jabin's army, which was led by a man named Sisera. Barak said to her, "I will go if you go with me. But if you do not go with me, I will not go." And Deborah replied, "For sure I will go with you. But the honor will not be yours as you go on your way. For the Lord will sell Sisera into the hands of a woman" (Judges 4:8–9 NLV).

* *

Dear Lord, Deborah was an amazing leader to serve as the only female judge of the nation of Israel and courageously fight enemy armies. I know You can do great things through me too. Amen.

36

GOD GATHERS THE WATERS OF THE SEA

[God] is faithful in all He does. He loves what is right and good and what is fair. The earth is full of the loving-kindness of the Lord. The heavens were made by the Word of the Lord. All the stars were made by the breath of His mouth. He gathers the waters of the sea together as in a bag. He places the waters in store-houses. Let all the earth fear the Lord. Let all the people of the world honor Him. For He spoke, and it was done. He spoke with strong words, and it stood strong.

PSALM 33:4–9 NLV

Have you ever sat on the beach, looking out and thinking how incredibly endless the ocean seems? Yet this psalm describes how God can gather the waters of the sea together as if He were simply putting something in a bag. Our one true God is so huge and powerful, so far beyond what our minds can imagine. Let that truth encourage you every single day— because the same huge and powerful God who handles the oceans so easily is the same God who can give you power and peace for whatever you are facing today.

- -

Dear God, I am amazed by Your greatness and power! If You can gather up the oceans and control them, I trust that You can bless me in amazing ways and help me with anything. Thank You! Amen.

YOU HAVE EXTRAS ON TOP

God will supply every need of yours according to his riches in glory in Christ Jesus. To our God and Father be glory forever and ever.
PHILIPPIANS 4:19–20 ESV

Frozen yogurt is so good, especially piled high with amazing toppings. Froyo is great on its own, but it's definitely even better with lots of extra little treats on top!

When you eat froyo, you can think about how God gives us good blessings and then often gives even more on top. When you're needing a mental boost in a hard situation, sometimes you need to take time to focus on the blessings you have and then the extra-special blessings God has piled on top. Write them down and pray over them with thanks. Showing gratitude for what God has done and what He has given you in the past is a great way to build hope and confidence for how He is going to supply your needs again right now and in the future!

· ·

Heavenly Father, thank You for blessing me so generously, even giving me extras on top of what I truly need. Thank You for all the ways You've provided for me and helped me in the past. I trust You for all the ways You will keep on giving and blessing in the future. Amen.

YOU HAVE THE MIDWIVES' EXAMPLE

*The king of Egypt said to the Hebrew midwives, whose names
were Shiphrah and Puah, "When you are helping the Hebrew
women during childbirth on the delivery stool, if you see
that the baby is a boy, kill him; but if it is a girl, let her live."
The midwives, however, feared God and did not do what the
king of Egypt had told them to do; they let the boys live.*

EXODUS 1:15–17 NIV

When Pharaoh, the Egyptian king, ordered that every new baby boy born
to God's people was to be killed, two of the midwives who helped moms
as they delivered their babies chose to respect God instead of Pharaoh.
They secretly defied Pharaoh (a very dangerous thing to do) and refused
to kill the baby boys. These women were named Shiphrah and Puah, and
we can follow their example of love and respect for God and human life
and their great courage.

*Heavenly Father, thank You for the example of Shiphrah
and Puah and the way they inspire me to be brave and
to love and respect You and human life. Amen.*

YOU HAVE JOCHEBED'S EXAMPLE

When she could hide him no longer, she got a papyrus basket for him and coated it with tar and pitch. Then she placed the child in it and put it among the reeds along the bank of the Nile. His sister stood at a distance to see what would happen to him.

EXODUS 2:3–4 NIV

One of the Israelite babies Shiphrah and Puah saved was Moses, and his mother's name was Jochebed. When it got harder and harder for her to keep hiding baby Moses as he grew bigger, she showed great courage and clever thinking. She came up with a plan to put Moses in a basket in the river near where the Egyptian princess liked to bathe. Jochebed hoped that the princess would find Moses and take care of him and keep him safe from the evil Pharaoh who wanted to kill all baby boys. And that's exactly what happened. Moses was safe and could grow up to be the great leader God planned for him to be!

* *

Dear God, thank You for the example of Jochebed. Please help me to have courage and think in clever ways like she did. Amen.

YOU HAVE MIRIAM'S EXAMPLE

Then his sister asked Pharaoh's daughter, "Shall I go and get one of the Hebrew women to nurse the baby for you?" "Yes, go," she answered. So the girl went and got the baby's mother.

EXODUS 2:7–8 NIV

Maybe you babysit or you've had to help watch over younger siblings, but probably not quite like Miriam in the Bible did. After her mother, Jochebed, came up with the idea to put baby Moses in a little basket in the river near where the Egyptian princess liked to bathe, Miriam helped make sure baby Moses stayed safe. She was the one to speak up when the princess discovered Moses. Miriam asked the princess if she wanted her to find someone to feed the baby until he was old enough to eat on his own and then go live with the princess. Her courageous action helped save Moses' life, plus he got to stay with his family a little longer.

. . . .

Father Lord, thank You for the blessing of Miriam's example. Please help me to do a good job looking out for those younger than me whenever I am needed. Amen.

GOD GIVES THE BEST MAKEOVERS

Therefore, I urge you, brothers and sisters, in view of God's mercy, to offer your bodies as a living sacrifice, holy and pleasing to God—this is your true and proper worship. Do not conform to the pattern of this world, but be transformed by the renewing of your mind. Then you will be able to test and approve what God's will is—his good, pleasing and perfect will.

ROMANS 12:1–2 NIV

God wants to give you an incredible makeover when you trust in Jesus as your Savior and choose to follow Him. He wants to change your life and your mind in the best kind of way! You should ask Him every day to help you not to act like the sinful people of this world. Ask Him to give you a mind like His, to help you see things the way He does and do the things He wants you to do. Ask Him to give you love, joy, peace, patience, kindness, goodness, faithfulness, gentleness, and self-control. Ask Him to help you grow in grace and truth and to help you serve and care for others so that others will want to know Him as Savior too!

. . . .

Dear Lord, please give me the best kind of makeover— the new life and mind You want for me, with thoughts and actions that align with Yours. Amen.

YOU ARE BLESSED WITH FORGIVENESS

The LORD is compassionate and merciful, slow to get angry and filled with unfailing love. He will not constantly accuse us, nor remain angry forever. He does not punish us for all our sins; he does not deal harshly with us, as we deserve. For his unfailing love toward those who fear him is as great as the height of the heavens above the earth. He has removed our sins as far from us as the east is from the west.

PSALM 103:8–12 NLT

If someone treats you badly again and again and again, it can be really hard to forgive them. So think about how awesome it is that God forgives us endlessly even though we all mess up a lot. We hurt our relationship with God when we don't acknowledge our sin and ask for His forgiveness. But as soon as we admit our sins and ask God to take them away, He does—as far as the east is from the west, actually! And then we can draw close to God and His goodness once again.

• •

Heavenly Father, no one forgives like You do! I'm so grateful for Your compassion, because I need Your mercy and forgiveness often. Remind me to admit my sins to You and let You take them far, far away. Thank You! Amen.

YOU ARE BLESSED BY AMAZING GRACE

Well then, should we keep on sinning so that God can show us more and more of his wonderful grace? Of course not! Since we have died to sin, how can we continue to live in it?

ROMANS 6:1–2 NLT

Since God forgives so fully and so well, sometimes we might think it's no big deal to keep doing anything we want, even if it's sinful, and then just ask for forgiveness, since God loves to forgive. But that mindset is wrong. If we truly love God, we want to obey Him and honor Him, not keep choosing sin with a "who cares?" attitude. We are certainly going to mess up and make bad choices sometimes, but we should feel regret about how those choices hurt God, and then we should do our best to avoid more sin in the future. Also, even though God always forgives when we ask, He doesn't always keep us from the consequences that go along with sin. We all need to ask God to help us keep running away from sin, never play around with it like it doesn't matter.

. . . .

Dear Lord, thank You for Your amazing, generous grace. Knowing You love and forgive me time and again gives me hope and peace. But I don't want to purposefully sin against You or pretend it's no big deal. Please continually strengthen my resolve to turn away from sin. Amen.

YOU ARE BLESSED BY THE LITTLE THINGS

"There is a boy here who has five barley loaves and two fish,
but what are they for so many?" Jesus said, "Have the people sit
down."... So the men sat down, about five thousand in number.
Jesus then took the loaves, and when he had given thanks, he
distributed them to those who were seated. So also the fish, as
much as they wanted. And when they had eaten their fill, he told
his disciples, "Gather up the leftover fragments, that nothing may
be lost." So they gathered them up and filled twelve baskets with
fragments from the five barley loaves left by those who had eaten.
JOHN 6:9–13 ESV

Think about what a great thing Jesus did with a small act of generosity from a young boy who gave up his lunch. It might not seem like too big of a deal, but the boy probably was a little worried he might not get to eat that day! And then Jesus did an amazing miracle, taking that little lunch and feeding a huge crowd of people with many baskets left over. Think about how many of those people must have believed in Jesus that day after seeing such a stunning miracle. Be faithful even in the smallest things God calls you to do. Who knows how He will bless you and show you miracles because of your obedience and generosity?

* *

Heavenly Father, I want to be faithful to You even in
the little things You ask of me. Show me how You want
to bless and reward me for doing so. Amen.

YOUR TIMES ARE IN GOD'S HANDS

But as for me, I trust in You, O Lord. I say,
"You are my God." My times are in Your hands.
PSALM 31:14–15 NLV

You may feel stressed about the future and plans for after high school. Or maybe you're stressed because you can't seem to decide on any good plans. Or maybe you're just trying not to worry at all and taking things day by day. Whatever the case, never stop talking to God and asking for His leading and His help in setting goals in your life. You are so blessed that, like the psalmist says in Psalm 31, your times are in God's hands. Ask Him to give you wisdom in all things and to open the right doors of opportunity for you—the ones that He knows are best for you to walk through, that match up with His will for your life and the good things He has planned for you to do. Remember that He sees and knows everything that is going on with you. He is loving and taking care of you in every situation.

. . . .

Heavenly Father, thank You that I can trust that my times
are in Your hands. Nothing anyone says or does against
me can change the fact that You are my God who holds
me, protects me, and takes good care of me. Amen.

YOU CAN BE KIND TO THE POOR

*Oh, the joys of those who are kind to the poor! The L**ORD**
rescues them when they are in trouble. The L**ORD** protects
them and keeps them alive. He gives them prosperity in the
land and rescues them from their enemies. The L**ORD** nurses
them when they are sick and restores them to health.*

PSALM 41:1–3 NLT

In what ways are you kind to the poor? God's Word promises that you
will be blessed and have joy when you care for the needy of this world.
Hopefully you're part of a Bible-teaching church that cares about poor
people and ministers to them. Are you joining in those efforts? Even in
your school and activities right now, who is needy? Maybe you can think
of people who are not just lacking financially but lacking in encouragement and friendship. How can you help? You might not have money to
give, but what are other ways you can lend a hand or show kindness?

*Heavenly Father, there are so many needs in the world these
days that trying to help can feel completely overwhelming.
Please help me not to grow discouraged. Instead, I pray that
You would help me give and serve with joy. Show me the
specific ways You want me to help the poor and needy around
me in my school, activities, church, and community. Amen.*

EVEN IF YOU SUFFER, YOU ARE BLESSED

Who is going to harm you if you are eager to do good? But even if you should suffer for what is right, you are blessed. "Do not fear their threats; do not be frightened." But in your hearts revere Christ as Lord. Always be prepared to give an answer to everyone who asks you to give the reason for the hope that you have. But do this with gentleness and respect, keeping a clear conscience, so that those who speak maliciously against your good behavior in Christ may be ashamed of their slander. For it is better, if it is God's will, to suffer for doing good than for doing evil.

1 PETER 3:13–17 NIV

Sometimes you do the right thing and suffer for it, while the one who did wrong seems to win. In those times, it's easy to feel bitter—but God wants you to feel blessed. He wants you to remember He's watching and He cares. He knows when you are suffering and whether or not you are faithful in the midst of it. He wants you to expect hard times and be prepared to honor and praise Him and point others to Him in the midst of them. What's more, He promises He will greatly reward you for your faithfulness.

Father God, help me never to feel bitter but always to feel blessed. No hard time that I go through here on earth can ever keep me away from Your goodness and gifts, which You give me in Your perfect timing when I am faithful to You. Amen.

YOU ARE BLESSED WHEN YOU STAND FIRM

Therefore, my dear brothers and sisters, stand firm. Let nothing move you. Always give yourselves fully to the work of the Lord.
1 CORINTHIANS 15:58 NIV

God doesn't want us to be wishy-washy and weak in our faith. He wants us to stand firm, like the apostle Paul describes in this scripture. We aren't supposed to let anything move us. We need to regularly evaluate if we have stuff going on in our lives that keeps us from standing firm and tempts us to move away from God. Any bad habits or activities that aren't honoring to God that we need to ditch? Any sins we are holding on to? Are we giving ourselves fully to God and the good works He has planned for us? That's how we keep ourselves standing firm and unmovable in our faith.

Heavenly Father, I want my life to be blessed because I stand firm in my faith in You and in my willingness to do whatever work You ask of me. Please help me rid my life of anything that weakens my relationship with You. Amen.

THE BLESSING OF WISDOM, PART 1

Joyful is the person who finds wisdom, the one who gains understanding. For wisdom is more profitable than silver, and her wages are better than gold. Wisdom is more precious than rubies; nothing you desire can compare with her. She offers you long life in her right hand, and riches and honor in her left. She will guide you down delightful paths; all her ways are satisfying. Wisdom is a tree of life to those who embrace her; happy are those who hold her tightly.

PROVERBS 3:13–18 NLT

Wanting wisdom isn't really considered cool these days, is it? Wisdom is often thought of as old and gray, not young and trendy. But it's a blessing to be wise—to be able to judge right from wrong, to use caution and good sense, and to stay away from sin—no matter what the world says is popular. And you can be wise right now, even as a teen. God's Word says, "If any of you lacks wisdom, you should ask God, who gives generously to all without finding fault, and it will be given to you" (James 1:5 NIV). There's no age requirement in that scripture, so ask God to give you wisdom and then use it and see all the blessings that come your way.

* *

Dear Lord, I ask You for wisdom, and I believe what Your Word says about its benefits and blessings. Please help me to inspire others my age to want Your wisdom and to use it in their lives too. Amen.

THE BLESSING OF WISDOM, PART 2

But when you ask, you must believe and not doubt, because the one who doubts is like a wave of the sea, blown and tossed by the wind. That person should not expect to receive anything from the Lord. Such a person is double-minded and unstable in all they do.

JAMES 1:6–8 NIV

It's important to remember not just to ask for God's wisdom and then do nothing else. Once you ask, you can be strong in faith and fully expect God to give it as He has promised. Then you need to use that wisdom to make your decision or take your next step or stay out of trouble or run away from sin. . .whatever your circumstances might be. When we're doubtful toward God and His wisdom, we become wishy-washy and unsteady, and we're easily tossed around by bad advice or the popular ideas of this world—and such doubt comes with a strong warning that we'll never receive blessings from God.

Father God, I don't want to doubt You. I know You alone are worthy of all my trust, and I want to be strong and confident in You. I want to use the wisdom and guidance You give me. Please help me to stand firm in my faith. Amen.

EVERYTHING WILL BE PERFECT ONE DAY

After you have suffered for awhile, God Himself will make you perfect. He will keep you in the right way. He will give you strength. He is the God of all loving-favor and has called you through Christ Jesus to share His shining-greatness forever. God has power over all things forever.

1 PETER 5:10–11 NLV

A perfect life here on earth would be so nice. But you know it's just not possible. You know there are all kinds of troubles and hurts in this world: little ones like a bad grade and big ones like the loss of a loved one. But God's Word promises that suffering and pain are just for a little while in this world as we wait for perfection forever in heaven. Meanwhile, God will keep you on the right path and give you strength to deal with the hard things of this life. None of them can ever overpower you because you trust that God has power over all of them.

• •

Heavenly Father, I hate the hurt in this world, but I love that You have complete power over all of it. I trust that You are working to make all things perfect and pain-free forever in heaven, for me and all who trust in Your Son, Jesus. Amen.

GOD KEEPS YOU STEADY

If you had not helped me, Lord, I would soon have gone to the land of silence. When I felt my feet slipping, you came with your love and kept me steady. And when I was burdened with worries, you comforted me and made me feel secure.

PSALM 94:17–19 CEV

If you live in an area where winter is long and cold, you surely know the feeling of your feet slipping. Ice and snow make everything slick, and you have to be extra careful not to fall. Or if you do fall, you want to make sure you have a big pile of soft snow to land in! When you read Psalm 94, you can think of that slippery feeling but then picture God's strong hand reaching out to steady you and keep you safe. In any slippery situation, you can remember that God is always ready to reach out His hand and help you.

* *

Heavenly Father, thank You for being the one who steadies me and holds me up. Thank You for comforting me and making me feel secure. Amen.

YOU HAVE THE DISCIPLES' EXAMPLE

One day as Jesus was walking along the shore of the Sea of Galilee, he saw two brothers—Simon, also called Peter, and Andrew—throwing a net into the water, for they fished for a living. Jesus called out to them, "Come, follow me, and I will show you how to fish for people!" And they left their nets at once and followed him. A little farther up the shore he saw two other brothers, James and John, sitting in a boat with their father, Zebedee, repairing their nets. And he called them to come, too. They immediately followed him, leaving the boat and their father behind.

MATTHEW 4:18–22 NLT

When Jesus started His ministry here on earth, He wanted close friends to come alongside Him, travel with Him, learn from Him, and help people believe in Him. These close friends were called His disciples. Think of what courage and faith it must have taken for them to leave the jobs they had known as fishermen to suddenly begin a whole new life with Jesus!

. . . .

Dear Jesus, help me to follow the examples of the disciples. If You call to me, I want to be ready to drop everything and do whatever You ask! Amen.

YOU CAN BE A BLESSING TO OTHERS AND TO JESUS

"'Come, you who are blessed by my Father, inherit the Kingdom prepared for you from the creation of the world. For I was hungry, and you fed me. I was thirsty, and you gave me a drink. I was a stranger, and you invited me into your home. I was naked, and you gave me clothing. I was sick, and you cared for me. I was in prison, and you visited me.' Then these righteous ones will reply, 'Lord, when did we ever see you hungry and feed you? Or thirsty and give you something to drink? Or a stranger and show you hospitality? Or naked and give you clothing? When did we ever see you sick or in prison and visit you?' And the King will say, 'I tell you the truth, when you did it to one of the least of these my brothers and sisters, you were doing it to me!'"

MATTHEW 25:34–40 NLT

Maybe some days you don't feel very close to Jesus but you'd like to be. You can draw closer to the Lord quickly and simply by helping someone in need, for Jesus told us that whenever we care for someone who is hungry or thirsty, sick or in need, it's like we're serving and blessing Jesus Himself. There's no better way to be close to Him!

Dear Jesus, never let me forget what a blessing it is to help and serve those in need. Sharing Your compassion and love with others is the best way to draw close to You. Amen.

ENCOURAGEMENT AND BRAVERY

Encourage each other and build each other
up, just as you are already doing.
1 Thessalonians 5:11 NLT

Think of a time when you really needed some extra encouragement and then received it. Maybe your parents surprised you with that new thing you'd been wanting but didn't need. Maybe a card came in the mail "just because." Maybe someone took you out for ice cream just for fun. Maybe a teacher noticed how hard you worked on a project and celebrated with you in class. Whatever it was, think of how it made you feel. Encouragement fills you with happiness and confidence. Also, notice that the word *courage* is in the word *encouragement*. When someone encourages you, their support helps you feel brave too—brave to face anything because you know you have people who love and care about you and cheer you on.

So next time you encourage someone in even the simplest way, and when you receive any kind of encouragement, think about how encouragement doesn't just bring joy—which is great, of course—but also helps others be brave to face any hard thing.

• •

Heavenly Father, thank You for the encouragers in my
life, and help me to be an encourager too. Amen.

THE LORD IS YOUR LIGHT

The Lord is my light and the One Who saves me. Whom should I fear? The Lord is the strength of my life. Of whom should I be afraid? When sinful men, and all who hated me, came against me to destroy my flesh, they tripped and fell. Even if an army gathers against me, my heart will not be afraid. Even if war rises against me, I will be sure of You. One thing I have asked from the Lord, that I will look for: that I may live in the house of the Lord all the days of my life, to look upon the beauty of the Lord, and to worship in His holy house. . . . I will sing. Yes, I will sing praises to the Lord.

PSALM 27:1–4, 6 NLV

You never have to fear the dark—literal darkness or figurative darkness. God is your light and your strength, and He is worthy of all your praise. You don't have to worry about the unknown because He knows it, and He saves you from any hidden dangers.

. . . .

Dear Lord, thank You that You are light, and You are my light. There is no darkness with You and nothing is hidden from or unknown by You. You save me and give me strength and courage so I don't have to fear anyone or anything. Amen.

YOU CAN LOOK AT JESUS, NOT THE STORM

*Peter answered him, "Lord, if it is you, command me to come
to you on the water." He said, "Come." So Peter got out of
the boat and walked on the water and came to Jesus.*

MATTHEW 14:28–29 ESV

Once when Jesus went off to pray alone, the disciples were in a boat
traveling on ahead of Him. Then in the middle of the night, He walked
out on the lake to catch up with them. The Bible says the disciples were
terrified. But Jesus immediately said to them, "It's me! Don't be afraid."
We can be assured that Jesus understands that even as we grow ever
closer to Him, we will sometimes struggle with fear. When we do, He will
always remind us that He is near. As soon as the disciple Peter realized
Jesus was the one out on the lake, he wanted to walk on water too. And
he trusted in Jesus' ability to make it happen. So he climbed out of the
boat and started walking miraculously on the waves toward Jesus. But
then something changed, and he began to sink. Peter had taken his focus
off of Jesus and put it on the wind and waves instead. The same thing
will happen to us if we're not careful. We must keep looking to Jesus
through every hard thing. If we do, He'll bless us and keep us steady. If
we don't, we'll begin to sink.

*Dear Jesus, I want to look at You, not at the storms in life. Please help
me to keep my focus on You and Your power to do anything! Amen.*

THE TRUTH AND GOODNESS OF GOD'S WORD

Every word of God has been proven true. He is a
safe-covering to those who trust in Him.
PROVERBS 30:5 NLV

Memorizing scripture is a powerful way to stay encouraged. God loves to bring verses to your mind exactly when you need them. Sometimes repeating a calming scripture, like Psalm 23, in your mind can help you to relax your breathing when you feel panicky. Sometimes singing praises like Psalm 136 is exactly what you need to have joy or combat the fear creeping up on you. Sometimes a powerful scripture that recounts the faith of others and the miracles of God, like Hebrews 11, is just what you need to grow your faith that God can do any kind of miracle in your situation too. Keep filling your mind with God's Word every chance you get, and see how He uses it to guide you and care for you and protect you.

. . . .

Heavenly Father, I'm so blessed by Your powerful Word. Please
bring specific verses and passages to my mind exactly when
I need them so I can keep my focus fixed on You! Amen.

YOU CAN GIVE AND BE BLESSED

"Bring all the tithes into the storehouse so there will be enough food in my Temple. If you do," says the LORD of Heaven's Armies, "I will open the windows of heaven for you. I will pour out a blessing so great you won't have enough room to take it in! Try it! Put me to the test! Your crops will be abundant, for I will guard them from insects and disease. Your grapes will not fall from the vine before they are ripe," says the LORD of Heaven's Armies. "Then all nations will call you blessed, for your land will be such a delight," says the LORD of Heaven's Armies.

MALACHI 3:10–12 NLT

Through the prophet Malachi, God encouraged the people of Israel to see how much He would bless them when they were obedient in giving their tithes and offerings to Him. We can remember this in our own lives. God calls us to give and loves when we give cheerfully (2 Corinthians 9:7). And Jesus said, "Give, and you will receive. Your gift will return to you in full—pressed down, shaken together to make room for more, running over, and poured into your lap. The amount you give will determine the amount you get back" (Luke 6:38 NLT).

Heavenly Father, I don't want to be selfish. I want to be generous. Please remind me of Your promises of blessing and help me to be a cheerful giver. Amen.

BLESSED BY WHAT YOU SAY (AND WHAT YOU DON'T SAY), PART 1

Watch your tongue and keep your mouth shut,
and you will stay out of trouble.
PROVERBS 21:23 NLT

God's Word is pretty direct about being careful with what we say. We all know it can be hard to control our tongues. Sometimes we talk back and dole out insults and tease too much. It's especially difficult to watch our words when we're angry or upset or feeling hurt or mistreated by someone. That's why it's important to focus on scriptures that remind us of how we are blessed when we hold our tongues and choose our words carefully. Scriptures like these:

- "Some people make cutting remarks, but the words of the wise bring healing" (Proverbs 12:18 NLT).

- "A gentle tongue is a tree of life, but a sinful tongue crushes the spirit" (Proverbs 15:4 NLV).

- "If you want to enjoy life and see many happy days, keep your tongue from speaking evil and your lips from telling lies" (1 Peter 3:10 NLT).

Dear Lord, please set a guard over my mouth and watch over the door of my lips (Psalm 141:3). I want to be careful with my words and honor You with them. Amen.

BLESSED BY WHAT YOU SAY (AND WHAT YOU DON'T SAY), PART 2

Let the words of my mouth and the thoughts of my heart be pleasing in Your eyes, O Lord, my Rock and the One Who saves me.
PSALM 19:14 NLV

So when you're doing well and controlling your tongue and holding back all those words you want to say but are choosing not to, what do you do with them? Give them to God! Remember that He already knows them anyway (Psalm 139:4). Express to Him all your frustrated and angry feelings. He tells us in His Word to give all our anxiety to Him because He cares for us (1 Peter 5:7). He wants us to pray about everything (Philippians 4:6), and we can ask Him to replace the angry and awful words we want to say with His peace and positivity instead. We can let Him give us wisdom to know what words to say and when to say them when we find ourselves in conflict and difficult conversations.

* *

Dear Lord, help me to remember to control my tongue and talk to You about all the things I want to say but shouldn't. Please give me peace and wisdom to know what to say and when I should say it. Amen.

THOSE WHO HAVE NOT SEEN

But [Thomas] said to them, "Unless I see the nail marks in his hands and put my finger where the nails were, and put my hand into his side, I will not believe." A week later his disciples were in the house again, and Thomas was with them. Though the doors were locked, Jesus came and stood among them and said, "Peace be with you!" Then he said to Thomas, "Put your finger here; see my hands. Reach out your hand and put it into my side. Stop doubting and believe." Thomas said to him, "My Lord and my God!" Then Jesus told him, "Because you have seen me, you have believed; blessed are those who have not seen and yet have believed."

JOHN 20:25–29 NIV

We can relate to Thomas sometimes. He just wanted to see in person, with his own eyes, that Jesus was alive. And Jesus blessed Thomas by coming to him. Yet Jesus also said, "Blessed are those who have not seen and yet have believed"—that includes you and me, and it encourages us to keep the faith.

• •

Dear Jesus, I can't deny that it's hard sometimes to keep my faith since I didn't get to be there in Bible times and see You with my own eyes. Yet I do believe You are alive and You love me. You have shown me Your presence in my life through the Holy Spirit. You are the one and only Savior. No one else is like You, Lord, and I love You! Amen.

GOD CAN MAKE IT GOOD

Joseph replied, "Don't be afraid of me. Am I God, that I can punish you? You intended to harm me, but God intended it all for good. He brought me to this position so I could save the lives of many people. No, don't be afraid. I will continue to take care of you and your children." So he reassured them by speaking kindly to them.

GENESIS 50:19–21 NLT

God can take the very worst of situations and turn it upside down. He can take anyone's evil plans toward you and work them out for your good. Consider the story of Joseph. It doesn't get much worse than being sold by your siblings into slavery in another country. Yet read the whole story of Joseph's life and look at the way God blessed Joseph through that awful experience. Whatever you're going through today, no matter how hard it is, choose to be loyal and obedient to God like Joseph was, and in His perfect timing God will surely bless you for your faithfulness.

· ·

Heavenly Father, thank You for Joseph's true story in the Bible to inspire and encourage me to keep being faithful to You even in the very worst of circumstances and injustice. You can take anything that's meant to be bad for me and turn it into good. I believe that, and I trust You! Amen.

YOUR GOD IS TRULY THE GREATEST

*Have you never heard? Have you never understood? The L*ORD*
is the everlasting God, the Creator of all the earth. He never
grows weak or weary. No one can measure the depths of his
understanding. He gives power to the weak and strength to the
powerless. Even youths will become weak and tired, and young
men will fall in exhaustion. But those who trust in the L*ORD *will
find new strength. They will soar high on wings like eagles. They
will run and not grow weary. They will walk and not faint.*

ISAIAH 40:28–31 NLT

You've probably heard of some athletes being called a GOAT—the greatest
of all time. But even the very best "goats" get tired and need their sleep.
They don't have endless energy and strength, no matter how much they
run and lift weights and train. Only the one true God never becomes
weary or weak, and this scripture in Isaiah can encourage you when you
do feel weak. Pray to Him and wait for Him. He is your source of true
energy and strength.

. . . .

*Almighty God, thank You that even though I get tired
and weak, You never do, and You give me new energy
and strength exactly when I need it. Amen.*

YOU CAN HONOR GOD

Do you not know that your bodies are temples of the Holy Spirit, who is in you, whom you have received from God? You are not your own; you were bought at a price. Therefore honor God with your bodies.
1 Corinthians 6:19–20 NIV

Always remember how blessed you are as a child of God, and take good care of yourself and the body God has given you! Ask Him every day to help you make healthy and wise choices. Because if you have asked Jesus to be your Savior, the Holy Spirit lives in you—and that makes your body a house for the Holy Spirit! The Bible says you are not your own but you belong to God. That's a good thing—the very best thing, actually!—because no one loves or cares for you like God does.

* *

Father God, thank You that I belong to You! Thank You for living in me! Please help me to take care of my body the best I can so that as You live in me I can do the good things You have planned for me. Amen.

BE HUMBLE, BE A SERVANT, BE BLESSED

When [Jesus] had finished washing their feet, he put on his clothes and returned to his place. "Do you understand what I have done for you?" he asked them. "You call me 'Teacher' and 'Lord,' and rightly so, for that is what I am. Now that I, your Lord and Teacher, have washed your feet, you also should wash one another's feet. I have set you an example that you should do as I have done for you. Very truly I tell you, no servant is greater than his master, nor is a messenger greater than the one who sent him. Now that you know these things, you will be blessed if you do them."

JOHN 13:12–17 NIV

Jesus is King of all kings and Lord of all lords, the one to whom everyone on earth will bow down one day. At the same time, He is truly a humble servant leader, as He demonstrated when He washed His disciples' feet. And He instructed them that they should do likewise and they would be blessed for being humble, obedient servants of each other. That message was not just for the disciples; it's for us today too.

• •

Jesus, thank You for showing us humility and compassion and service and love. I want to be like You and treat others like You do. Amen.

GLORY TO GOD FOREVER

Oh, the depth of the riches of the wisdom and knowledge of God! How unsearchable his judgments, and his paths beyond tracing out! "Who has known the mind of the Lord? Or who has been his counselor?" "Who has ever given to God, that God should repay them?" For from him and through him and for him are all things. To him be the glory forever! Amen.

ROMANS 11:33–36 NIV

This scripture reminds you how truly awesome God is! No one can ever fully understand Him. Does that mean you shouldn't even try? No way! He shows so much of Himself to you through His Word, through His creation, through His people, and on and on! Everything comes from Him and is made for Him and is held together by His great power. He wants you to keep getting to know Him better and better and to keep experiencing His amazing love for you.

• •

Almighty God, I worship You! You are truly extraordinary, awesome, and amazing! I want to take time every day to focus on how wonderful You are and how blessed I am to call You my heavenly Father! Amen.

YOU HAVE THE BEST ROLE MODEL

*We can be sure that we know Him if we obey His teaching.
Anyone who says, "I know Him," but does not obey His teaching
is a liar. There is no truth in him. But whoever obeys His Word
has the love of God made perfect in him. This is the way to
know if you belong to Christ. The one who says he belongs
to Christ should live the same kind of life Christ lived.*

1 JOHN 2:3–6 NLV

When you look up to someone, like a famous athlete or cool celebrity, you admire certain things about who that person is and what they do. Wanting to follow that person or be like them might help give you some good goals for your life, but to have a truly blessed life means you choose to look to Jesus as your most important model, above and beyond all others. God the Father sent His Son, Jesus Christ, to earth to be a human being just like all of us and to be our example for living the best and most blessed kind of life. And how do we do that? By reading and studying God's Word to keep learning more and more about who God is and how Jesus lived.

* *

*Dear Jesus, You are my very best role model and my perfect
example of how to live. Please help me to love learning
about and growing in You and Your ways. Amen.*

YOU ARE BLESSED WHEN YOU REST

[God] rested on the seventh day from all His work which He had done.
GENESIS 2:2 NKJV

Do you remember being little and hating to take naps? Did you give your parents fits about them? How do you feel about sleep these days? Maybe you wish you didn't need it at all, because you have so much to do and not enough time in the day. Or maybe sleep is your favorite hobby, and you'd spend a lot more time snoozing in your bed or on the couch if you could. Either way, God blesses us with rest. Our minds and bodies need it, and it's important to make good time for it. Spiritually, we need it too, and we find true spiritual rest in Jesus Christ alone. He said, "Come to me, all of you who are weary and carry heavy burdens, and I will give you rest. Take my yoke upon you. Let me teach you, because I am humble and gentle at heart, and you will find rest for your souls. For my yoke is easy to bear, and the burden I give you is light" (Matthew 11:28–30 NLT).

. . . .

*Dear Jesus, thank You for giving me the peace
and rest that my soul longs for. Amen.*

YOU HAVE ESTHER'S EXAMPLE

Esther sent this reply to Mordecai: "Go, gather together all the Jews who are in Susa, and fast for me. Do not eat or drink for three days, night or day. I and my attendants will fast as you do. When this is done, I will go to the king, even though it is against the law. And if I perish, I perish."

ESTHER 4:15–16 NIV

If you know the story of Esther in the Bible, you know she had extraordinary courage to help save her people from an evil man in a high royal position in the land of Persia. Take time to read the whole book of Esther, and then anytime you're needing some extra faith and courage, ask God to remind you of Esther's great faith and courage and how He worked out His good plans to protect His people through her. He can do incredible things like that through you too, if you are willing to let Him.

. . . .

Father God, thank You for Esther's example. I want to be bold and brave like her to do the good things You have planned for me. Amen.

YOU BELONG TO GOD

We know that we are children of God and that the world around us is under the control of the evil one. And we know that the Son of God has come, and he has given us understanding so that we can know the true God. And now we live in fellowship with the true God because we live in fellowship with his Son, Jesus Christ. He is the only true God, and he is eternal life.

1 JOHN 5:19–20 NLT

You might wonder sometimes why bad things happen in this world. It's because people sin, and the whole world is under the power of our enemy, the evil one, also called the devil or Satan. But those of us who believe in Jesus as Savior belong to God, so the evil one can never defeat us. Satan can attack us and hurt us, but God gives us life that lasts forever, no matter what! We should never want to follow any type of false god who will lead us into the ways of the evil one. Only the one true God leads us to life that lasts forever.

* *

Heavenly Father, I'm so blessed and grateful that I belong to You! Please show me and protect me from everything that is bad, and help me to keep away from false gods. I trust that because Jesus is my Savior, You give me life that lasts forever! Amen.

72

A BIG GOAL

I will be careful to live a life without blame. When will You come to me? I will walk within my house with a right and good heart. I will set no sinful thing in front of my eyes. I hate the work of those who are not faithful. It will not get hold of me. A sinful heart will be far from me. I will have nothing to do with sin.

PSALM 101:2–4 NLV

It's not popular in this world to say you will have nothing to do with sin. A lot of people would say that's dumb and that it's no big deal to play around a little with bad choices and disobedience to God's Word. So it's a big goal to say like the psalmist does in this passage that you want nothing to do with sin. And it's an *awesome* goal. Jesus took all sin away from us when He died on the cross, and that is grace, but now we should never want to act like sin is no big deal. Because Jesus had to die to save us from sin, we should recognize how serious and awful sin is and want to avoid it as much as possible.

* * *

Dear Lord, please show me every day the sins I need to get rid of in my life. I don't ever want to play around with them, and I know the more I stay away from sin, the more I experience Your blessings. When I do mess up, I'm so sorry. I trust that You forgive me because of Jesus, and I am grateful! Amen.

YOU HAVE ANNA'S EXAMPLE

Anna, a prophet, was also there in the Temple. She was the daughter of Phanuel from the tribe of Asher, and she was very old. Her husband died when they had been married only seven years. Then she lived as a widow to the age of eighty-four. She never left the Temple but stayed there day and night, worshiping God with fasting and prayer. She came along just as Simeon was talking with Mary and Joseph, and she began praising God. She talked about the child to everyone who had been waiting expectantly for God to rescue Jerusalem.

LUKE 2:36–38 NLT

Anna was a woman of the Bible who, after losing her husband, devoted her life to worshipping and praying to God and speaking His Word in the temple. She was extremely close to God. When Jesus' parents brought Him to the temple as an infant, she praised God and told anyone who would listen that Jesus was the promised Savior.

Father God, help me to remember Anna's example and share Your Word every chance I get. I want to help people know that Jesus is our one and only Savior. Amen.

BLESSED TO BE LIKE CHILDREN

People were bringing little children to Jesus for him to place his hands on them, but the disciples rebuked them. When Jesus saw this, he was indignant. He said to them, "Let the little children come to me, and do not hinder them, for the kingdom of God belongs to such as these. Truly I tell you, anyone who will not receive the kingdom of God like a little child will never enter it." And he took the children in his arms, placed his hands on them and blessed them.

MARK 10:13–16 NIV

You're growing up and becoming an adult fast. As you look to the future, what are the things you're looking forward to about not being a kid anymore? What are the things you will miss? It's fun to hold on to childhood in some ways, even while it's good and necessary to grow and mature. We can be glad, then, that God's Word tells us a way we should always be childlike—in the way we receive His kingdom. As little kids, we don't usually worry and fret about too much. We're pretty carefree and eager and enthusiastic. We have great love for and faith in our parents or the ones who take care of us. And in that same kind of way, our heavenly Father wants us to remain like children forever—trusting in Him completely to provide for every single one of our needs and eagerly enjoying His great love for us.

. . . .

Heavenly Father, even as I'm growing up, help me to always have childlike, enthusiastic love and joy and faith in You. Amen.

SO BLESSED TO BE SAVED

*As he was approaching Damascus on this mission, a light from
heaven suddenly shone down around him. He fell to the ground
and heard a voice saying to him, "Saul! Saul! Why are you
persecuting me?" "Who are you, lord?" Saul asked. And the voice
replied, "I am Jesus, the one you are persecuting! Now get up
and go into the city, and you will be told what you must do."*

ACTS 9:3–6 NLT

The apostle Paul (previously called Saul) in the Bible was saved in an exceptionally dramatic way when God called him out of his life of darkness and destruction. You can read the whole account in Acts 9. Our stories of coming to faith in Jesus probably aren't quite as dramatic as Paul's, yet they are still just as important and meaningful. Faith in Jesus Christ as our Savior and Lord is the greatest gift we could ever receive. We are saved from the devastating effects of sin in our lives because Jesus took all the punishment upon Himself. His sacrificial love for us is so amazing, so awesome! We have every reason to give Him thanks and praise!

* *

*Jesus, I praise You and thank You endlessly
for saving me from sin. Amen.*

IT'S BETTER TO GIVE THAN TO RECEIVE

*"I have never coveted anyone's silver or gold or fine clothes.
You know that these hands of mine have worked to supply my
own needs and even the needs of those who were with me. And
I have been a constant example of how you can help those in
need by working hard. You should remember the words of the
Lord Jesus: 'It is more blessed to give than to receive.'"*

ACTS 20:33–35 NLT

These are the apostle Paul's words in the book of Acts, and we should
learn from them and want to mimic them in our own lives today. We
should never jealously want expensive things that others have. Instead,
we should be willing to work as God makes us able, to provide for our
own needs and the needs of those who aren't as fortunate as we are.
We should remember those words straight from Jesus that it's better
to give than to receive. How are you accepting and applying this lesson
in your own life?

• •

*Lord Jesus, it's a struggle not to be jealous of cool things that
other people have that I don't. So please help me to keep my focus
on Your words and Your will for my life. Help me to work hard
with the abilities You've given me and to obey You and remember
what a blessing it is to be generous and bless others. Amen.*

YOU HAVE THE STRENGTH TO FACE ANYTHING

Christ gives me the strength to face anything.
PHILIPPIANS 4:13 CEV

Have you ever really, really wanted to quit something? Maybe you wished you could drop out of a class at school because it felt way too hard. Or maybe you tried a new sport but didn't want to finish the season. We've all been there. But when we do finish a semester or a season without quitting, sometimes we can look back and see how God was giving us just the right amount of courage and strength and blessing to take things one day at a time. And hopefully we can see how He used that time to grow us into better, stronger people because we endured instead of giving up. In any hard situation, be sure to call on God for help; then trust in Him and wait on Him. He will either help you walk through it day by day until it's over or help you find a wise way out immediately.

• •

Father God, please help me when I want to quit in a hard situation.
Please bless me with endurance, courage, and wisdom. Amen.

GOD'S VOICE AND POWER AND PEACE

*The voice of the LORD echoes above the sea. The God of glory
thunders. The LORD thunders over the mighty sea. The voice of the
LORD is powerful; the voice of the LORD is majestic. The voice of
the LORD splits the mighty cedars; the LORD shatters the cedars of
Lebanon.... The voice of the LORD strikes with bolts of lightning.
The voice of the LORD makes the barren wilderness quake; the
LORD shakes the wilderness of Kadesh. The voice of the LORD
twists mighty oaks and strips the forests bare.... The LORD rules
over the floodwaters. The LORD reigns as king forever. The LORD
gives his people strength. The LORD blesses them with peace.*
PSALM 29:3–5, 7–11 NLT

Think of the loudest, deepest, most powerful voice you've ever heard. But
the loudest voice in all the world can never have power like God's voice
does. Let this scripture from Psalm 29 encourage you. Read it, remember
it, and trust in it—and let it grow your faith in our extraordinary God.
With just His voice He can say and do anything at all. No matter what is
going on in the world, God is always in control, always able to use His
voice to help and rescue in the good ways He chooses.

• •

*Almighty God, remind me of the power of Your incredible
voice that is able to do anything at all! Amen.*

EVERY BLESSING

Every good and perfect gift is from above, coming down from the Father of the heavenly lights, who does not change like shifting shadows.

JAMES 1:17 NIV

You are so blessed every day by the many things, both big and little, that you possess. Each one is a blessing from God. "Wait, what?" you might say. "My parents pay for our house and food, and they bought me my phone; my friend gave me this bracelet; and I bought this outfit with my own money." But 1 Corinthians 4:7 (NLT) says, "What do you have that God hasn't given you? And if everything you have is from God, why boast as though it were not a gift?"

Yes, you may receive gifts from family members and buy things with your own money, but who gives each person life and the ability to work and earn money and pay for things? God does. Ultimately, every good thing comes from Him!

Job in the Bible said, "We bring nothing at birth; we take nothing with us at death. The LORD alone gives and takes. Praise the name of the LORD!" (Job 1:21 CEV).

* *

Heavenly Father, I want to remember every single moment that every good thing in my life ultimately comes from You! Thank You for providing for me and blessing me so generously! Amen.

NEW BLESSINGS

There is one who is free in giving, and yet he grows richer.
And there is one who keeps what he should give, but he
ends up needing more. The man who gives much will have
much, and he who helps others will be helped himself.

PROVERBS 11:24–25 NLV

God wants us to hold not tightly but *lightly* to the things He has given us. We can't open our hands to receive new gifts from God if we don't let go of the things He has already given us. Our hands can't hold everything at once. Neither can our lives! So we are called to give and give and then give some more, and to be amazed by the ways God gives us new blessings.

* *

Heavenly Father, please help me to always have a generous spirit, not a selfish and greedy one. I trust that You are the one who provides for me and blesses me in all the ways I need and that are good for me to enjoy. I know You want me to share and bless others with what You've given me. Everything I have is ultimately Yours. I give it back to You, and I'm so grateful for all I constantly receive from You! Amen.

LIFE AND BREATH AND EVERYTHING

"[God] himself gives everyone life and breath and everything else."
ACTS 17:25 NIV

It's not just material possessions that God blesses you with. It's every good thing—even the very next breath you take. Simply being alive and having opportunities to grow and learn and serve Jesus as You follow Him is the best blessing ever. Even if you feel like you are lacking in some way today—maybe there's something new you wish you had or an opportunity you wish would come your way—instead of focusing on what you don't have, how can you fix your thoughts on all the good things and opportunities you do have? What is God asking you to do with your gifts and your abilities and your life? How might He bring new blessings to you when you're obedient and faithful and grateful for what you already have?

· ·

Dear Lord, please forgive me when I'm greedy and ungrateful. Help me to focus on all that You bless me with every single day. Just being alive is an incredible blessing. Thank You for my life and my possessions and my opportunities. I want to use them to serve You and show my love for You! Please guide and direct me. Amen.

BLESSED ARE THOSE WHO FEAR THE LORD

Blessed are those who fear the LORD, who find great delight in his commands. Their children will be mighty in the land; the generation of the upright will be blessed. Wealth and riches are in their houses, and their righteousness endures forever. Even in darkness light dawns for the upright, for those who are gracious and compassionate and righteous. Good will come to those who are generous and lend freely, who conduct their affairs with justice. Surely the righteous will never be shaken; they will be remembered forever. They will have no fear of bad news; their hearts are steadfast, trusting in the LORD. Their hearts are secure, they will have no fear.

PSALM 112:1–8 NIV

The blessing in this psalm is something every Christian should long for. Those who fear the Lord and are happy to obey His commands are the ones who have the promise of God's care and blessing. He doesn't want bad attitudes; He wants us to enjoy obeying Him because following His commands is the best way to live a good life here on earth and later a perfect life in heaven. Loving and obeying God makes us truly blessed, both now and forever.

• •

*Heavenly Father, thank You for Your good commands.
I always want to be happy to obey them! Amen.*

YOU HAVE RAHAB'S EXAMPLE

Joshua the son of Nun sent two men from Shittim to go in secret to learn about the land. He said to them, "Go and spy out the land, and Jericho." So they went and came to the house of Rahab.

JOSHUA 2:1 NLV

If you read about Rahab in the Bible, you will learn how she had great courage to help two men whom Joshua (the leader of the Israelite people after Moses died) sent into the land of Canaan to spy on the city of Jericho. The men came to her house, but then someone found out and warned the king that they were spies. So Rahab helped the two spies hide. And she told them that she trusted in their God and asked them to help protect her family when they came into the land of Canaan to take it over. The spies promised they would if she didn't tell anyone about their plans. Then Rahab let them down by a rope through the window and told them to hide for three days in the hill country before returning home. Later, by that same red rope, the spies knew where to find her and her family to protect them from being killed when the Israelites took over Jericho.

. . . .

Heavenly Father, please help me to remember Rahab's example and have courage to trust You and help others. Amen.

BLESSED BY LIMITS

I will set no sinful thing in front of my eyes.
PSALM 101:3 NLV

These days everyone seems to be online and on their phones all the time. Having access to so much information and so many cool ways to interact with people is amazing in many ways, but there's a whole lot of awful junk online too. You constantly need to ask God for wisdom and set healthy limits on Internet and social media use. We all do, at every age. You also need to have courage to look away and do something else if friends are pressuring you to spend time online in ways you know are wrong or have been told are off-limits by your parents. This can be hard, especially when it feels like so many others have no limits online. But stay strong. There are many good and God-honoring things to do instead!

* *

Heavenly Father, please help me to set limits and look away from unhealthy, sinful things online. The world is connected through the Internet, but I'll be extra blessed when I'm careful and disconnect in healthy ways too. Amen.

YOU HAVE A MERCIFUL GOD

*Have mercy on me, LORD, for I am in distress. Tears blur
my eyes. My body and soul are withering away. I am
dying from grief; my years are shortened by sadness.*
PSALM 31:9–10 NLT

It's okay to cry. Maybe you've gotten yourself into trouble and you're
not sure how to get out. Maybe a "frenemy" is being mean to you all the
time. Maybe right now school just seems way too hard. Maybe a loved
one has died or a close friend has moved away. In those times when you
feel like you'll never stop crying, be sure to cry out to God. He loves you
and He is full of mercy toward you. The writer of this psalm goes on to
tell God, "How great is the goodness you have stored up for those who
fear you. You lavish it on those who come to you for protection, blessing
them before the watching world. You hide them in the shelter of your
presence, safe from those who conspire against them. You shelter them
in your presence, far from accusing tongues. Praise the LORD, for he
has shown me the wonders of his unfailing love" (Psalm 31:19–21 NLT).

· ·

*Heavenly Father, I trust You and Your love and mercy. Please
show me that You care about my sadness and struggles, and
give me help and comfort to get through them. Amen.*

AUTHENTIC BEAUTY

*Don't be concerned about the outward beauty of fancy hairstyles,
expensive jewelry, or beautiful clothes. You should clothe yourselves
instead with the beauty that comes from within, the unfading
beauty of a gentle and quiet spirit, which is so precious to God.*

1 PETER 3:3–4 NLT

No matter what anyone tries to tell you or what social media photos try
to show you, authentic beauty comes from the inside, not what anyone
looks like on the outside. Your heart—the way you treat others and share
God's kindness and love in the ways His Word teaches—is what makes
you truly gorgeous. If you have a gentle and quiet spirit, it means you are
listening for God's voice and leading in your life and you put your hope
in Him. That's the kind of beauty that never fades and always ages well.

• •

*Heavenly Father, please help me not to focus on outer appearance
but on real, authentic inner beauty that shines out of me
and inspires others to want to know You more! Amen.*

YOU ARE NEVER ALONE

God has said, "I will never fail you. I will never abandon you." So we can say with confidence, "The LORD is my helper, so I will have no fear. What can mere people do to me?"

HEBREWS 13:5–6 NLT

In a scary situation, it always feels worse to be on your own. That's why it's so important to remember that you are never, ever totally alone. God has promised that He never leaves you! He is your helper at all times. You might have family and friends who love you and love to help you, but no person can promise what God promises! You can trust Him and call out to Him in any kind of trouble—day or night, no matter where you are—and have peace knowing that He is more powerful than anything that could happen to you. He loves you and rescues you!

* *

Father God, thank You for being with me in every situation. I'm so grateful You never leave me alone. I don't want to forget Your constant presence. Amen.

YOU SHOULD KEEP ON ASKING

Jesus told his disciples a story about how they should keep on praying and never give up: In a town there was once a judge who didn't fear God or care about people. In that same town there was a widow who kept going to the judge and saying, "Make sure that I get fair treatment in court." For a while the judge refused to do anything. Finally, he said to himself, "Even though I don't fear God or care about people, I will help this widow because she keeps on bothering me. If I don't help her, she will wear me out." The Lord said: Think about what that crooked judge said. Won't God protect his chosen ones who pray to him day and night? Won't he be concerned for them? He will surely hurry and help them.

LUKE 18:1–8 CEV

Jesus gave us this example of a woman being persistent to teach us to be persistent in prayer. The point is that if a judge in the courts who did not even respect God was finally willing to help the woman who kept asking and asking, how much more will God help His people who keep asking for His help?

• •

Heavenly Father, I'm so thankful that You never get tired of my prayers. You want me to keep on asking and asking and asking for Your help. Amazing! Amen.

LET GOD HANDLE IT

When someone does something bad to you, do not pay him back with something bad. Try to do what all men know is right and good. As much as you can, live in peace with all men. Christian brothers, never pay back someone for the bad he has done to you. Let the anger of God take care of the other person. The Holy Writings say, "I will pay back to them what they should get, says the Lord."
ROMANS 12:17–19 NLV

It's super hard to do, but when we're mistreated, we're far better off to let God handle it than to try to handle it ourselves. God loves us so much more than even our very best family and friends. We can trust Him to take care of our needs and bring justice when we've been wronged. That doesn't mean we have to be doormats who get walked all over. And it doesn't mean God never asks us to do something to stand up for ourselves. It means we humbly ask for God's help and seek His plan for true justice. We ask Him to guide us and tell us when to speak up and when to be quiet, when to act and when to be still. God sees and knows everything, and He gets angry at injustice too! His goodness and justice will always prevail, not always on the timeline we'd like but always according to His perfect schedule.

. . . .

Dear Lord, please calm me down and guide me. Help me to let You handle any kind of mistreatment I experience. Amen.

HOLDING YOU UP

*"Don't be afraid, for I am with you. Don't be discouraged,
for I am your God. I will strengthen you and help you.
I will hold you up with my victorious right hand."*

ISAIAH 41:10 NLT

Have you ever been so sick or in so much pain that you couldn't even hold yourself up? Maybe someone had to carry you or let you lean on them. In those moments, the support you feel is God's love shown to you through the people who are helping. When you look back and think about those hard times and the people God provided to help, you can look forward and not be afraid of anything that might happen today or in the future. You can trust that God will provide exactly the people and things you need to deal with any difficulty or heartache that is to come.

. . . .

*Father God, thank You for being with me and blessing me. Thank
You for encouraging me, strengthening me, and helping me with
everything. Thank You for holding me up. Thank You for all the ways
You provide for me and care for me, and I especially thank You for the
wonderful people You put in my life who show me Your love. Amen.*

BLESSED BY THE PROMISE KEEPER

And the LORD gave them rest on every side just as he had sworn to their fathers. Not one of all their enemies had withstood them, for the LORD had given all their enemies into their hands. Not one word of all the good promises that the LORD had made to the house of Israel had failed; all came to pass.

JOSHUA 21:44–45 ESV

We are so blessed to love and worship the one God who is the true promise keeper. Time and again the Bible shows how God kept His promises to His people. The accounts of God's faithfulness in the Bible remind us that He keeps His promises to His people today as well. That includes you if you have accepted Jesus Christ as your Savior. The more you read God's Word, the more you learn about the many promises of God and how blessed you are because of them.

. . . .

Father God, thank You for making and keeping Your promises to all of Your people, including me. Please help me to learn more and more about Your promises and to grow stronger and more confident in my faith as I do. Help me to share about Your promises with others too. Amen.

GOD PROMISES THAT YOU CAN FIND HIM

"You will seek me and find me when you seek me with all your heart."
JEREMIAH 29:13 NIV

True, we don't have God here in human form these days, and it sure must have been amazing to have learned from Jesus when He lived on earth. (Can you picture yourself as one of Jesus' followers back then? It's fun to imagine!) But today we have the Holy Spirit present with us and we have God's Word to teach and guide us. We have God's promises that we can find Him (Deuteronomy 4:29) and that He is never far from us (Acts 17:27). If we ever feel that God is far away or we can't find Him, we need to consider what our attitudes and actions and habits have been like lately. Have we been holding on to any sin that we need to let go and seek forgiveness for? Have we been spending regular time with God through His Word and in prayer? James 4:8 (NLT) says, "Come close to God, and God will come close to you. Wash your hands, you sinners; purify your hearts, for your loyalty is divided between God and the world."

. . . .

Father God, thank You that You don't hide away from me. You want to be found and You want to be close to me. Help me to get rid of anything in my life that creates distance from You. Amen.

GOD PROMISES TO HELP AND PROTECT YOU

I will lift up my eyes to the mountains. Where will my help come from? My help comes from the Lord, Who made heaven and earth. He will not let your feet go out from under you. He Who watches over you will not sleep. Listen, He Who watches over Israel will not close his eyes or sleep. The Lord watches over you. The Lord is your safe cover at your right hand. The sun will not hurt you during the day and the moon will not hurt you during the night. The Lord will keep you from all that is sinful. He will watch over your soul. The Lord will watch over your coming and going, now and forever.
PSALM 121 NLV

What are you needing God's help for today? It could be anything! Sometimes it's a smaller thing, like understanding your homework or finding your missing cell phone. Sometimes it's a big thing, like dealing with mean girls or grieving the death of a loved one. Or maybe you feel unsafe and desperately long for protection. Almighty God promises both to help you and to keep you safe, and you can trust Him to keep His promises.

- -

Heavenly Father, thank You for Your help and protection in every situation. Every person who helps me, everything that works out, every bit of safety I have ultimately comes from You as You watch over my life and care for me. I'm so grateful to be Your child, now and forever. Amen.

GOD PROMISES HIS COMFORT

God is our merciful Father and the source of all comfort. He comforts us in all our troubles so that we can comfort others. When they are troubled, we will be able to give them the same comfort God has given us. For the more we suffer for Christ, the more God will shower us with his comfort through Christ. Even when we are weighed down with troubles, it is for your comfort and salvation!

2 CORINTHIANS 1:3–6 NLT

Imagine a totally trouble-free life. What a dream world that would be! And absolute fiction until heaven because hard times and troubles are unavoidable in this life. But when we go through them, we have the awesome promise that God will comfort us. Not only that, but there is purpose in our troubles and in our comfort, because we can use our experiences to comfort and help others. We may even lead others to salvation in Jesus Christ! Think back to ways you have felt God's comfort or are feeling it now. Then praise God and plan how you can help share comfort with others. Keep up the awesome cycle of receiving and giving God's comfort—until the day we'll finally have no more troubles or tears ever again (Revelation 21:4).

Father God, I thank You for all the ways You comfort me and bring me peace, even in the worst of troubles. Help me to remember that comfort well and pass it along to others while sharing with them about Your love and salvation. Amen.

YOU CAN HAVE PERFECT PEACE

*You will keep in perfect peace those whose minds are steadfast,
because they trust in you. Trust in the LORD forever, for the LORD,
the LORD himself, is the Rock eternal. . . . The path of the righteous is
level; you, the Upright One, make the way of the righteous smooth.
Yes, LORD, walking in the way of your laws, we wait for you; your
name and renown are the desire of our hearts. My soul yearns
for you in the night; in the morning my spirit longs for you.*

ISAIAH 26:3–4, 7–9 NIV

Perfect peace almost sounds *way* too good to be true, doesn't it? There always seems to be something stressing us out, even if it's just a sibling squabble or an annoying classmate or a huge homework assignment. But God's Word tells us how to have perfect peace—by trusting in God and fixing our thoughts on Him. When we feel our peace being disrupted, we need to turn our attention back to God and ask for His help to handle what's causing the stress.

* *

*Heavenly Father, I trust You and would love to have perfect
peace all the time. In stressful situations, please help me to
turn my thoughts back to You and keep them there! Amen.*

DISCIPLINE IS A BLESSING

Blessed is the one you discipline, LORD,
the one you teach from your law.
PSALM 94:12 NIV

Yes, discipline really is a blessing, no matter how much we don't enjoy it. The Bible states very clearly that no one enjoys discipline while it's happening, but later "it produces a harvest of righteousness and peace for those who have been trained by it" (Hebrews 12:11 NIV). You can see this principle at work in other areas of your life. If you're disciplined in doing your homework and studying, there's a payoff of good grades and new knowledge and skills learned. If you're disciplined in sports or arts or music, there's a payoff in how you perform and create. Far more important than the good disciplines of this world are the ways God is spiritually disciplining us to grow in our faith and obedience to Him. We should "endure hardship as discipline; God is treating you as his children," Hebrews 12:7 (NIV) tells us. And "God disciplines us for our good, in order that we may share in his holiness" (Hebrews 12:10 NIV).

• •

Heavenly Father, help me to remember how much I matter to You. You
discipline me with love because of the good things You are doing in
and for me, so that I can be closer to You and more like You. Amen.

YOU KNOW THE BEST PROMISE KEEPER

"God is not human, that he should lie, not a human being, that he should change his mind. Does he speak and then not act? Does he promise and not fulfill? I have received a command to bless; he has blessed, and I cannot change it."

NUMBERS 23:19–20 NIV

Think of a time someone made a promise to you and then couldn't keep it. You can probably think of a time when you let someone down that way too. But God will never break a promise. He is the only one who can make a perfect promise and the only one who can always *keep* His perfect promises. He is not human, and He cannot lie or make mistakes. When He speaks, His Word is always right and true. Even the very best people who love you the most will sometimes let you down, even if they don't mean to—because they are human. But God is above and beyond us, and you can trust Him completely.

• •

Heavenly Father, I'm so blessed to know You, the very best promise keeper! I want to keep reading Your Word and learning about all of Your amazing promises to those who love You. Amen.

YOU HAVE THE ARMOR OF GOD

Put on every piece of God's armor so you will be able to resist the enemy in the time of evil. Then after the battle you will still be standing firm. Stand your ground, putting on the belt of truth and the body armor of God's righteousness. For shoes, put on the peace that comes from the Good News so that you will be fully prepared. In addition to all of these, hold up the shield of faith to stop the fiery arrows of the devil. Put on salvation as your helmet, and take the sword of the Spirit, which is the word of God.

EPHESIANS 6:13–17 NLT

Do you have certain clothes you like to wear because when you put them on, you instantly feel more confident to face anything in your day? A favorite outfit that you know looks good and feels good too? An athlete ready to play feels most confident and brave with her uniform on and her gear in top shape. And a soldier going to battle absolutely needs protective armor. God tells us that we as Christians need to be equipped as well—and He provides us with a special kind of spiritual armor to wear as we fight the spiritual battles going on around us at all times.

. . . .

Dear Lord, thank You for blessing and equipping me with spiritual protective armor that is exactly what I need to be strong, courageous, and ready to fight against evil. Amen.

GOD'S LOVE IS UNFAILING

The steadfast love of the Lord never ceases;
his mercies never come to an end.

LAMENTATIONS 3:22 ESV

When was the last time you acted like a selfish brat? We all do at times, unfortunately! It's amazing that even on our worst days, when our worst attitudes and thoughts and actions are on display and we're feeling the most miserable and unlovable, God sees and knows them all yet still loves us endlessly. His love is steadfast and unfailing, and He promises it always will be. He proved His amazing love for us in this way: "While we were still sinners, Christ died for us" (Romans 5:8 NIV). He knew exactly how awful we can be in our sin, and still He loved and died for us. What an incredible blessing to have such a faithful Savior!

. . . .

Father God, even though You see the very worst of me, You love me unconditionally, and I could never thank You enough. I want Your steadfast, unfailing love to inspire me to live my life the best way I can, avoiding sin as much as I possibly can. You know I won't live life perfectly, but as I try my best, You will continue to love me and help me grow in goodness and grace. I am so grateful! Amen.

YOU HAVE ANGELS WATCHING OVER YOU

"See that you do not despise one of these little ones.
For I tell you that in heaven their angels always
see the face of my Father who is in heaven."
MATTHEW 18:10 ESV

Maybe you hear people talk about guardian angels sometimes and wonder if they are real or not. There are all kinds of fictional stories about angels, of course, but what really matters is what God's Word says about them. Check out these scriptures and realize how blessed you are that God gives you mighty protection and care through angels all the time:

- "The angel of the Lord encamps around those who fear him, and delivers them" (Psalm 34:7 ESV).
- "[God] will command his angels concerning you to guard you in all your ways" (Psalm 91:11 ESV).
- "Are [angels] not all ministering spirits sent out to serve for the sake of those who are to inherit salvation?" (Hebrews 1:14 ESV).

Heavenly Father, thank You for angels! I ask You to guard and protect me well through them. It's amazing to realize that You provide supernatural care for me through them. My heart overflows with gratitude! Amen.

GOD WILL GIVE YOU YOUR HEART'S DESIRES

Don't. . .envy those who do wrong. For like grass, they soon fade away. Like spring flowers, they soon wither. Trust in the LORD and do good. Then you will live safely in the land and prosper. Take delight in the LORD, and he will give you your heart's desires. Commit everything you do to the LORD. Trust him, and he will help you.

PSALM 37:1–5 NLT

Sometimes it's hard not to envy the ones who do wrong and who don't follow God. In this world it often seems like they're the ones having all the fun. It seems like you should just go along with whatever seems popular, even if deep down you know that what's popular is not right. So it takes huge courage to ignore and avoid sinful people, especially if you're feeling pressure from people who on the surface seem to be your friends. But God promises if you trust Him and do good, you will have everything you need plus much more, because He will bless you for committing yourself to Him.

. . . .

Heavenly Father, I commit myself to You above all. Please help me to ignore and avoid those who do wrong. I want to do the good and right things that make You happy. Amen.

GOD LIVES IN YOU

God has given us his Spirit as proof that we live in him and he in us. Furthermore, we have seen with our own eyes and now testify that the Father sent his Son to be the Savior of the world. All who declare that Jesus is the Son of God have God living in them, and they live in God. We know how much God loves us, and we have put our trust in his love. God is love, and all who live in love live in God, and God lives in them.

1 JOHN 4:13–16 NLT

What are you feeling anxious about today? So many sad and stressful and scary things are happening in this world, but be assured that you are never left to face any of them alone! When you believe that Jesus is the one true Savior and the Son of God, then God is living in you through His Holy Spirit, and you are living with His constant love and help. There's no better blessing than that!

* *

Heavenly Father, I believe in Jesus as my Savior, and so I need to remember that You are with me always to help with any hard thing. Sometimes I forget, and I'm sorry. Please fill me up with awesome hope and peace and courage as I trust that You live in me and never leave me. Amen.

LOTS AND LOTS OF MONEY

*The love of money is a root of all kinds of evil. Some
people, eager for money, have wandered from the
faith and pierced themselves with many griefs.*

1 TIMOTHY 6:10 NIV

Having plenty of money and not needing to worry much about your finances or budget can be a huge blessing. But if we find ourselves to be so fortunate, we have to be very, very careful. First Timothy 6:17–19 (NIV) gives special instruction to the wealthy, saying, "Command those who are rich in this present world not to be arrogant nor to put their hope in wealth, which is so uncertain, but to put their hope in God, who richly provides us with everything for our enjoyment. Command them to do good, to be rich in good deeds, and to be generous and willing to share." Our goals in life shouldn't center on making lots of money. Instead we should focus on asking God for His will to be done in our lives. If He does happen to bless us with wealth, that's awesome—and we then get to be good stewards who are very generous with our wealth for His glory and to help spread the gospel of Jesus Christ.

* *

*Heavenly Father, thank You for providing for me financially. Please
give me wisdom about money and wealth. I know everything
ultimately comes from You, and I want to use whatever You
bless me with to please You and point others to You. Amen.*

EVEN THROUGH THE DARKEST VALLEY

*The Lord is my shepherd, I lack nothing. He makes me lie down
in green pastures, he leads me beside quiet waters, he refreshes
my soul. He guides me along the right paths for his name's sake.
Even though I walk through the darkest valley, I will fear no evil,
for you are with me; your rod and your staff, they comfort me.*

PSALM 23:1–4 NIV

You've probably walked through some dark valleys in your life, times
when you may have felt hurt by a friend or maybe even lost a loved one.
Or you might be feeling disappointed or dealing with a lot of worry and
fear. God never promises that you won't experience those hard things,
but He does promise He is close beside you as you go through them. It's
often during the worst and most painful moments that we feel God's
presence the closest. When you feel you're in a dark valley, ask God to
show you how close He is and how much He cares. He will answer you
in many ways and through many people and sources.

*Father God, You are always my source of love and light and blessing,
even through the deepest and darkest valleys. Thank You! Amen.*

STORM STOPPER

Soon a fierce storm came up. High waves were breaking into the boat, and it began to fill with water. Jesus was sleeping at the back of the boat with his head on a cushion. The disciples woke him up, shouting, "Teacher, don't you care that we're going to drown?" When Jesus woke up, he rebuked the wind and said to the waves, "Silence! Be still!" Suddenly the wind stopped, and there was a great calm. Then he asked them, "Why are you afraid? Do you still have no faith?" The disciples were absolutely terrified. "Who is this man?" they asked each other. "Even the wind and waves obey him!"

MARK 4:37–41 NLT

Can you imagine how terrified Jesus' disciples must have been during the storm described in Mark 4? Yet it took only a moment for Jesus to speak and make everything okay. Through the Holy Spirit, that same powerful, storm-stopping presence of Jesus is with you right now! Anytime you're in the middle of an actual weather storm or any circumstance of life that feels like a storm, you can call on Jesus to make a way through it for you.

· ·

Dear Jesus, help me to remember that You are the storm stopper. You are capable of simply speaking the words and stopping anything scary or stressful in my life. I'm so blessed that You are my Savior. Amen.

YOU CAN WORK HARD FOR THE LORD

Do not be lazy but always work hard. Work for
the Lord with a heart full of love for Him.
ROMANS 12:11 NLV

Do you have a good work ethic? Are you willing to work hard and do your best with the gifts and talents God has given you? A good work ethic doesn't mean you should never take a break or rest or just have some fun. Of course you should! But it's so easy to get lazy and take too many breaks and have too much rest and too much fun. When you have schoolwork to do, you can do your very best at it. When you have a job to do and things to take care of, you can work at those things eagerly and with a good attitude. Think of God Himself as the boss overseeing you, because ultimately He is, but He's the best kind of boss— full of love and blessing for you as you do the good work He sets before you.

· ·

Heavenly Father, I want to have a work ethic that shows others I work
to honor You most of all. Please help me to find great joy in my work.
You are so good to me, and I'm honored to do my best for You! Amen.

YOU CAN LOOK FORWARD WITH HOPE

*We should live in this evil world with wisdom, righteousness,
and devotion to God, while we look forward with hope
to that wonderful day when the glory of our great
God and Savior, Jesus Christ, will be revealed.*

TITUS 2:12–14 NLT

You should always be watching for Jesus to return. He promises He will, and His return will be incredible to see! It might sound rather scary because it will be unlike anything anyone has ever experienced, but it will be wonderful for everyone who loves and trusts Him. Mark 13:24–27 (nlv) says: "After those days of much trouble and pain and sorrow are over, the sun will get dark. The moon will not give light. The stars will fall from the sky. The powers in the heavens will be shaken. Then they will see the Son of Man coming in the clouds with great power and shining-greatness. He will send His angels. They will gather together God's people from the four winds. They will come from one end of the earth to the other end of heaven."

* *

*Dear Jesus, I'm watching and waiting for You to return
and gather Your people, including me! Your return is
going to be awesome! I love You and trust You. Amen.*

GOD IS WATCHING YOU

*The eyes of the Lord are in every place,
watching the bad and the good.*
PROVERBS 15:3 NLV

No one watches out for you like God does. The Bible says He sees and knows everything that happens in every place, all the time. "No one can hide from God. His eyes see everything we do. We must give an answer to God for what we have done," says Hebrews 4:13 (NLV). And Job 28:24 (NLV) says, "He looks to the ends of the earth, and sees everything under the heavens." For people who make a lot of bad choices, these verses might seem scary, but for those who love God and want to follow and obey His Word, they are hopeful and encouraging. God only wants you to obey His good ways because He loves you and wants what's best for you. When you trust that He is always watching out for you, you can have peace and confidence, knowing He's able to help in every moment.

• •

*Heavenly Father, please remind me that You are always
watching me—in every place and every moment.
Thank You for caring so much about me! Amen.*

YOU HAVE RUTH'S EXAMPLE

Ruth said, "Do not beg me to leave you or turn away from following you. I will go where you go. I will live where you live. Your people will be my people. And your God will be my God. I will die where you die, and there I will be buried. So may the Lord do the same to me, and worse, if anything but death takes me from you." When Naomi saw that Ruth would do nothing but go with her, she said no more to her.

RUTH 1:16–18 NLV

Ruth and Naomi's story is such a great example of the blessing of loyalty in our lives. Read the whole story of Ruth and you'll see how she had every reason to go do her own thing, but she promised to stick with Naomi no matter what. And then God blessed Ruth far more than she ever could have imagined. How are you exhibiting loyalty to others? Who are the loyal people in your life, and how are you showing them your love and loyalty and gratitude in return?

. . . .

Heavenly Father, thank You for the true story of Ruth and Naomi in Your Word to show me examples of loyalty. Please help me to be a loyal loved one to others, and thank You for the loved ones in my life who are so loyal to me. Amen.

YOUR GOD IS ALWAYS EVERYWHERE

*Where can I go from your Spirit? Where can I flee from your
presence? If I go up to the heavens, you are there; if I make
my bed in the depths, you are there. If I rise on the wings of
the dawn, if I settle on the far side of the sea, even there your
hand will guide me, your right hand will hold me fast. If I say,
"Surely the darkness will hide me and the light become night
around me," even the darkness will not be dark to you; the
night will shine like the day, for darkness is as light to you.*

PSALM 139:7–12 NIV

God is omnipresent, meaning He is in all places all the time. Everywhere
you go, He is with you. In good times and bad, He is right there, and you
can call out to Him for help or in worship or just to talk to Him about
anything. No person can ever promise you what God promises you. He
says, "I will never leave you or let you be alone" (Hebrews 13:5 NLV).

* *

*Heavenly Father, thank You for being in all places
all the time. I need You with me every moment,
and I'm so grateful You never leave me. Amen.*

YOU CAN GIVE GOD ALL THE CREDIT

The Scriptures say, "If you want to brag, then brag about the Lord." You may brag about yourself, but the only approval that counts is the Lord's approval.

2 CORINTHIANS 10:17–18 CEV

Of course you feel happy when you accomplish something cool, right? And that's great! We all do. We just can't forget to give God the ultimate credit for each and every good thing we do. He deserves every bit of praise and worship because He is the one who gives us our gifts and abilities. It's so important to stay humble and never be full of pride because James 4:6 (NLT) says, "God opposes the proud but gives grace to the humble," and James 4:10 says when we humble ourselves before God, He will lift us up in honor—and that's a far better blessing than anything our own selfish pride will gain for us!

. . . .

Heavenly Father, please forgive me when I'm prideful and bragging. You alone are worthy of all praise. Please remind me that it doesn't matter what others think about me; all that matters is what You think of me! I trust in Your grace and blessings. Amen.

YOU HAVE ZACCHAEUS' EXAMPLE

[Zacchaeus] was seeking to see who Jesus was.
LUKE 19:3 ESV

Zacchaeus was a wealthy man, a chief tax collector who lived in Jesus' time. Men like him were known for cheating and taking way too much of other people's money. So most people who knew Zacchaeus hated and avoided him.

But Zacchaeus was drawn to Jesus and wanted to do whatever it took to see Him as He traveled through Jericho. Even though Zacchaeus wasn't very tall and it would be hard for him to find a good view among the crowds of people, he was determined. He ran ahead of where Jesus would walk, and he climbed a big tree. Soon Jesus was near, and when He reached that tree, He stopped and spotted Zacchaeus. Then He called him by name and said, "Come down right away. I'm going to your house today."

Zacchaeus was amazed and excited. He climbed down immediately and welcomed Jesus to his home. As Zacchaeus spent time with Jesus, he was sorry for his sins. He wanted to make all his wrongs right. He wanted to help the poor. He wanted to give back to people all the money he had cheated them out of, plus four times more.

· ·

Heavenly Father, thank You for the example of Zacchaeus, who was determined to get close to Jesus and then admitted his mistakes and wanted to do all he could to make them right. I want to be a lot like Zacchaeus. Amen.

113

TREAT OTHERS WELL

Sympathize with each other. Love each other as brothers and sisters. Be tenderhearted, and keep a humble attitude. Don't repay evil for evil. Don't retaliate with insults when people insult you. Instead, pay them back with a blessing. That is what God has called you to do, and he will grant you his blessing. For the Scriptures say, "If you want to enjoy life and see many happy days, keep your tongue from speaking evil and your lips from telling lies. Turn away from evil and do good. Search for peace, and work to maintain it. The eyes of the LORD watch over those who do right, and his ears are open to their prayers. But the LORD turns his face against those who do evil."

1 PETER 3:8–12 NLT

God is watching everything we think and say and do as we interact with others. And He knows we all have a sin nature and can have plenty of conflict and difficult relationships sometimes. But when we're doing our best to treat others as this scripture instructs us, He promises His blessings to us.

. . . .

Dear Lord, please help me to be a loving and kind person. Help me to treat other people in my life the way this scripture from 1 Peter tells me to. I want to have good relationships, and most of all I want to have a good relationship with You and receive Your blessings! Amen.

WHAT ARE YOU BUILDING ON?

"Anyone who listens to my teaching and follows it is wise, like a person who builds a house on solid rock. Though the rain comes in torrents and the floodwaters rise and the winds beat against that house, it won't collapse because it is built on bedrock. But anyone who hears my teaching and doesn't obey it is foolish, like a person who builds a house on sand. When the rains and floods come and the winds beat against that house, it will collapse with a mighty crash."
MATTHEW 7:24–27 NLT

If you've ever gone to the beach, maybe you've seen some amazing sand-castles or even built some yourself. But we all know that a sandcastle never lasts for too long in the waves and weather. Jesus taught that it matters what you build on. Anything built on a strong foundation like rock is able to stand firm through all kinds of weather. If you build your life on the strong rock of Jesus and His Word, you will stand firm and brave through all kinds of situations. Jesus went on to say that anything built on sand is not strong enough to last. He was comparing people who hear His teaching and listen and obey it to people who only hear it but do nothing with it. Those who obey Jesus are built up strong for whatever life brings their way, while those who ignore Jesus are easily washed away.

· ·

Dear Jesus, I don't want to ignore You and be easily washed away. Please build me up with great faith as I depend on You to be my rock in every kind of weather! Amen.

KEEP ON

*Have pity, God Most High! My enemies chase me all day.
Many of them are pursuing and attacking me, but even when
I am afraid, I keep on trusting you. I praise your promises!
I trust you and am not afraid. No one can harm me.*
PSALM 56:1–4 CEV

What good is it if we just say we trusted God once, and that's it? We have to keep on trusting God, even when we're afraid, even when we're confused, even when we're angry, even when we're heartbroken, even when something very difficult is going on in our lives. We should want the constant action of choosing trust in God again and again each day, knowing we face new challenges and realizing that we need to focus on His perfect promises to guide us and protect us. The end of Psalm 56 goes on to say, "You protected me from death and kept me from stumbling, so that I would please you and follow the light that leads to life" (verse 13 cev).

* *

*Heavenly Father, again today I choose to keep on trusting
You! I want this to be my prayer every day! I'm so blessed
that You guide me with the light that leads to life. Amen.*

YOU ARE UNDER GOD'S PROTECTION

Live under the protection of God Most High and stay in the shadow of God All-Powerful. Then you will say to the LORD, "You are my fortress, my place of safety; you are my God, and I trust you." The Lord will keep you safe from secret traps and deadly diseases. He will spread his wings over you and keep you secure. . . . The LORD Most High is your fortress. Run to him for safety, and no terrible disasters will strike you or your home. God will command his angels to protect you wherever you go. They will carry you in their arms.
PSALM 91:1–4, 9–12 CEV

These powerful verses promise that God takes care of us if we live under His protection. So how do we do that? First, we trust Him as the one true God. We believe in Jesus as our only Savior. We do our best to follow God's Word and live according to it. We stay in close relationship with our heavenly Father. All of that is awesome anyway, plus we receive many gifts of God's loving care on top!

• •

Father God, thank You for Your precious promises to me in Psalm 91. I am so blessed by You! Amen.

YOU HAVE GREAT COMMANDMENTS TO OBEY

"Teacher, which is the most important commandment in the law of Moses?" Jesus replied, "'You must love the LORD your God with all your heart, all your soul, and all your mind.' This is the first and greatest commandment. A second is equally important: 'Love your neighbor as yourself.' The entire law and all the demands of the prophets are based on these two commandments."

MATTHEW 22:36–40 NLT

Jesus said the two most important commandments to obey are to love God first with all your heart, soul, and mind and to love your neighbor as yourself. If you make these your main priority in life, you will automatically do other things well too. Because as you love God with all your heart, soul, and mind, you'll be wanting to learn more and more about Him. And as you continually learn about Him and grow closer to Him plus love others as you love yourself, you'll find yourself living the wonderful life He has planned for you.

• •

Heavenly Father, I want to obey these greatest commandments above everything else in my life. Please help me to stay focused on them. Amen.

YOU CAN HAVE FAITH FROM AFAR

Jesus said to him, "Go your way. Your son will live."
The man put his trust in what Jesus said and left.
JOHN 4:50 NLV

The nobleman in John 4 had government authority over Jesus, but he respected Jesus. The nobleman came to Jesus and begged him to heal his sick son. And Jesus said, "Go your way. Your son will live." But that wasn't exactly what the nobleman wanted to hear. He thought surely Jesus needed to be present with his son to heal him. And with his authority, the nobleman could have ordered Jesus to do so. The nobleman had to decide if he could trust that Jesus could heal simply by saying the words from afar. The nobleman decided to believe Jesus had the miraculous power to heal from anywhere, and he trusted Jesus would do it. He took Jesus at His word and headed home.

While he was still traveling, some of his servants met him along the way, saying, "Your son is alive!" The nobleman was filled with joy and asked, "What time did he get better?"

The servants said, "His fever left him yesterday at the seventh hour." The father realized that was the exact time that Jesus had said to him, "Your son will live." From then on, not only did the nobleman believe in Jesus, but so did everyone in his household.

This story reminds us how blessed we can be when we take Jesus at His word and trust Him anywhere and anytime.

Dear Jesus, I choose to trust in You. Amen.

YOU DON'T NEED TO WHINE

God is working in you, giving you the desire and the power to do what pleases him. Do everything without complaining and arguing, so that no one can criticize you. Live clean, innocent lives as children of God, shining like bright lights in a world full of crooked and perverse people.

PHILIPPIANS 2:13–15 NLT

Whining is so obnoxious, isn't it? Yet we all do it sometimes, even if it's just in our heads. But we're far better off when we decide not to complain. If you choose to be happy and grateful in every situation where you're tempted to whine instead, think of how different your mindset will be. Think of how much more joy and peace you'll have. Think of how inspiring that joy and peace will be to others. Think of how contagious your attitude could be as you spread joy and peace to others. Then you can share the reasons for your joy and peace—salvation and life with Jesus Christ as Lord!

. . . .

Heavenly Father, thank You for working in me and giving me the power to do what makes You happy. Help me not to whine, complain, or argue in any situation but instead to have joy and gratitude because of all my blessings, especially the blessing of Jesus as my Savior. Amen.

YOU ARE NEVER TRAPPED

Fearing people is a dangerous trap, but
trusting the Lord means safety.
PROVERBS 29:25 NLT

Think about a time when you felt trapped. Maybe you were physically trapped or maybe you were stuck in a situation where it felt like there was no end to the stress or anxiety you were feeling. Proverbs 29:25 says that fearing people is a dangerous trap. We can get our minds stuck in a rut that we feel hopeless to break free from if we constantly fear other people—what they might do or even just what they think of us. So trusting God is where our safety and peace are. He is in control over all things and all people, and when we trust Him completely over everything else, He provides us with ultimate safety.

• •

Dear God, I want to fear only You, meaning I want to have a deep respect for You. I don't want to fear any other people or any hard situations. When I trust in You completely, I know You will keep me safe. Thank You for protecting and caring for me! Amen.

GOD'S POWER FOR YOU

I ask the glorious Father and God of our Lord Jesus Christ to give you his Spirit. The Spirit will make you wise and let you understand what it means to know God. My prayer is that light will flood your hearts and you will understand the hope given to you when God chose you. Then you will discover the glorious blessings that will be yours together with all God's people. I want you to know about the great and mighty power that God has for us followers. It is the same wonderful power he used when he raised Christ from death and let him sit at his right side in heaven.

EPHESIANS 1:17–20 CEV

In this scripture the apostle Paul is sharing his prayers with the Christians who lived in Ephesus. These same prayers are what God wants for you as a Christian today too. If you believe in Jesus as your only Savior, you belong to Him and are filled with hope at all the awesome things God has planned for you. And His power for you is so great—it is the same power that brought Jesus back to life! That incredible power is working in you now so that you can do the good things God wants for you, and it will be working in you forever because it has given you eternal life.

. . . .

Heavenly Father, help me to see and believe more every day how great You are, how awesome Your power is, and how much You love me. Amen.

YOU KNOW THE ONE TRUE RELIGION

We need such a Religious Leader Who made the way for man to go to God. Jesus is holy and has no guilt. He has never sinned and is different from sinful men. He has the place of honor above the heavens. Christ is not like other religious leaders. They had to give gifts every day on the altar in worship for their own sins first and then for the sins of the people. Christ did not have to do that. He gave one gift on the altar and that gift was Himself. It was done once and it was for all time.

HEBREWS 7:26–27 NLV

Many people say that all religions are the same and all roads lead to heaven, but that's just not true. Belief in Jesus as God and as our one and only Savior is what's true. Jesus alone was (and is) perfect and holy and without sin. He gave His own life once for all, for people of all time, and no other religion offers that kind of gift and love and miracle! To know Jesus as Savior is to believe in Him and accept His awesome gift of grace and the eternal life He provided when He took away our sins by dying on the cross for them and then rising to life again.

• •

Dear Jesus, no one else is like You! You are the one true God and Savior, and I'm so blessed that You've revealed Yourself to me! Amen.

YOU CAN HAVE A GOOD NAME

A good name is to be chosen instead of many riches. Favor is better than silver and gold. The rich and the poor meet together. The Lord is the maker of them all. A wise man sees sin and hides himself, but the foolish go on, and are punished for it. The reward for not having pride and having the fear of the Lord is riches, honor and life.

PROVERBS 22:1–4 NLV

A good name means a good reputation and good character. When people hear your name, what do you hope they think? Do you want them to think of you in good ways or bad? Do you want to be known for things like laziness or lying or being snobby or rude or getting into trouble? Or do you want to be known for things like doing your best and being honest, fair, kind, compassionate, and worthy of respect? When you live for God and follow His ways of true love and kindness and integrity, you will make and keep a good name for yourself. Best of all, you'll bring glory to His great name!

* *

Father God, I want to be known for good character qualities. Please help me to have a good name and most importantly to point others to knowing and honoring You. Amen.

WHEN YOU REMEMBER

Moses said to the people, "Remember this day in which you came out from Egypt, out of the house of slavery, for by a strong hand the LORD brought you out from this place."
EXODUS 13:3 ESV

Have you had bad things happen that you just want to forget because they were *so* awful and you're *so* glad they're over? We can all think of things like that. But to some extent we do need to remember them so that we never forget how God helped us get through them. It can be a blessing to look back on hard times and grow our faith to trust that God will continue to help us both now and in the future. Moses told the people of Israel to remember the amazing day that God finally brought them out of slavery in Egypt. Just like they did, we also need to remember all the incredible ways God has helped us endure and overcome bad experiences. He did help, He does help, and He always will help.

• •

Heavenly Father, I know that every bit of help and rescue I have ever received ultimately came from You! I never want to forget Your goodness, and I trust You to help me and rescue me again and again. I am so grateful for Your faithfulness! Amen.

YOU CAN SEE GOD EVERYWHERE IN CREATION

*What may be known about God is plain to them, because
God has made it plain to them. For since the creation of the
world God's invisible qualities—his eternal power and divine
nature—have been clearly seen, being understood from
what has been made, so that people are without excuse.*

ROMANS 1:19–20 NIV

God has shown Himself and His qualities through everything He has
made in creation, so no person on earth can say they know nothing about
God. He can be seen in the gorgeous little details of a flower and in the
vast expanse of stars in the clear nighttime skies. He can be seen in the
mind-blowing ways our human body systems are designed. He can be
seen in the ways animals know how to hunt for their food and care for
their young and build themselves homes. And that's to name just a few!
Our Creator God is awesome and worthy of all our praise, and we are
exceedingly blessed to call Him Father and Savior.

. . . .

*Almighty God, I love seeing Your qualities in all the things
You have made. Thank You for making Yourself known.
I pray that more people will want to grow closer to You
through Jesus because of seeing You in creation. Amen.*

WHILE YOU WAIT

*Wait for the LORD; be strong, and let your heart
take courage; wait for the LORD!*
PSALM 27:14 ESV

It's hard to be patient. We want that new thing or opportunity or relationship or result or answer to prayer right *now*, please and thank you! But goodness and blessing result from patience. Consider the following scriptures on this topic and look for more in His Word. Draw close to God and let Him teach you to wait well. "But they who wait for the Lord shall renew their strength; they shall mount up with wings like eagles; they shall run and not be weary; they shall walk and not faint" (Isaiah 40:31 esv).

- "The LORD is good to those who wait for him, to the soul who seeks him" (Lamentations 3:25 ESV).

- "But as for me, I will look to the LORD; I will wait for the God of my salvation; my God will hear me" (Micah 7:7 ESV).

- "Wait for the LORD and keep his way, and he will exalt you to inherit the land" (Psalm 37:34 ESV).

* *

*Heavenly Father, I need to do better at waiting well.
Help me to be a patient person who trusts in Your perfect
timing. Teach me the things I need to learn while I wait.
I believe in Your goodness and blessings. Amen.*

YOUR GOD KNOWS ALL

"For I am God, and there is no other. I am God, and there is no one like Me. I tell from the beginning what will happen in the end. And from times long ago I tell of things which have not been done, saying, 'My Word will stand. And I will do all that pleases Me.' . . . I have planned it, and I will do it."
ISAIAH 46:9–11 NLV

You are blessed that the God who loves you so dearly is omniscient. He is the one true know-it-all—and that's a good thing! Scripture tells us that God can tell from the beginning what will happen in the end. Sometimes we wish He would tell us everything He knows, but He wants us to trust Him day by day. He has good plans, and our job is to love and follow and worship and serve Him until one day we live with Him in heaven forever.

* *

Heavenly Father, I'm grateful that You know everything! You always have and always will. I trust Your goodness and Your plans! Please help me to keep on following You day by day. Amen.

YOU MIGHT GET MORE THAN YOU DREAMED

[Jesus] said to Simon, "Now go out where it is deeper, and let down your nets to catch some fish." "Master," Simon replied, "we worked hard all last night and didn't catch a thing. But if you say so, I'll let the nets down again." And this time their nets were so full of fish they began to tear! A shout for help brought their partners in the other boat, and soon both boats were filled with fish and on the verge of sinking.

LUKE 5:4–7 NLT

Jesus helped the fishermen catch far more than they could have imagined. They had just spent the whole night fishing and had caught nothing, but Jesus only had to say the words, and suddenly the fish were everywhere—enough to tear their nets and sink their boat! Never forget that God is able to bless you with so much more than you expect. Keep trusting Him, keep praising Him, keep waiting on His perfect timing, and keep asking Him for everything you need—and He just might provide so much more than you ever dreamed!

• •

Heavenly Father, so often You go above and beyond to show how You love to bless and care for Your people. Thank You for blessing me in above-and-beyond ways too! Amen.

GOD TURNS YOUR DARKNESS TO LIGHT

I will lead the blind in a way that they do not know, in paths that they have not known I will guide them. I will turn the darkness before them into light, the rough places into level ground. These are the things I do, and I do not forsake them.

ISAIAH 42:16 ESV

You might feel like you're stumbling around in the dark sometimes, like you just can't see the right way to go when you have a big choice to make or when you're facing a big problem. So trust this scripture where God promises to turn darkness into light and make rough places smooth for His people. He will help you see step-by-step. He will open up new paths for you when you don't know what to do or where to go. And He will never, ever leave you!

. . . .

Heavenly Father, I'm following You and Your light even when I can't see or understand exactly where You are taking me. I trust You to take me on good paths and to make all the rough spots smooth. Thank You for leading me and never leaving me. Amen.

NONE LIKE THE LORD

Among the gods there is none like you, Lord; no deeds can compare with yours. All the nations you have made will come and worship before you, Lord; they will bring glory to your name. For you are great and do marvelous deeds; you alone are God. Teach me your way, Lord, that I may rely on your faithfulness; give me an undivided heart, that I may fear your name. I will praise you, Lord my God, with all my heart; I will glorify your name forever.

PSALM 86:8–12 NIV

Do you ever stop to think about how awesome it is to know the one true God and to have a personal relationship with Him because of Jesus Christ (1 Timothy 2:4–6)? There is no one like Him in all the world. He alone is worthy of all your praise, so go ahead and praise Him for the privilege of being His child!

* *

Heavenly Father, You are so awesome and so good to me. Only You are the one true God, and I am so thankful to know You and be loved by You! I love You too, and I want to follow You and worship You forever. Amen.

YOU HAVE GOD'S PROTECTION

The first time I was brought before the judge, no one came with me. Everyone abandoned me. May it not be counted against them. But the Lord stood with me and gave me strength so that I might preach the Good News in its entirety for all the Gentiles to hear. And he rescued me from certain death. Yes, and the Lord will deliver me from every evil attack and will bring me safely into his heavenly Kingdom. All glory to God forever and ever! Amen.

2 TIMOTHY 4:16–18 NLT

Even when Paul had no one else to help, God Himself was with Paul and gave him strength. Paul trusted that God would protect him from every sinful plan or evil attack. And he knew someday God would bring him into heaven forever. Paul wrote these things in his letter to Timothy, but they are for you to remember today too. You are blessed to have God's mighty protection and the promise of safety in His heavenly kingdom!

* *

Heavenly Father, thank You for your mighty protection. I trust that no matter what happens here in this world, You will ultimately always keep me safe because someday You are going to bring me into perfect paradise in heaven to live with You forever! Amen.

YOU HAVE A GOOD SHEPHERD

[Jesus said,] "My sheep listen to my voice; I know them, and they
follow me. I give them eternal life, and they will never perish.
No one can snatch them away from me, for my Father has given
them to me, and he is more powerful than anyone else. No one can
snatch them from the Father's hand. The Father and I are one."
JOHN 10:27–30 NLT

We don't usually want to be called a farm animal, do we? But when we're considering the way Jesus calls us His sheep, it truly is a blessing. Jesus is our Good Shepherd, and we are His sheep. He cares for us, protects us, and provides for us so well that no one can ever separate us from God the Father, who holds us in His hand. We don't need to fear any earthly dangers or difficult circumstances or even death, for our true home is with Jesus in heaven where we will live forever in perfect peace.

. . . .

Lord Jesus, my Good Shepherd, I'm so grateful to be one of Your
sheep. Thank You for loving me, guiding me, protecting me, and
providing for me. Thank You for life and love that last forever. Amen.

YOU CAN PRAISE AND PRAY CONSTANTLY

I will honor the Lord at all times. His praise will always be in my mouth. My soul will be proud to tell about the Lord. Let those who suffer hear it and be filled with joy. Give great honor to the Lord with me. Let us praise His name together.

PSALM 34:1–3 NLV

We all get in trouble with our words. Maybe you too easily sass your parents or tease your siblings or get impatient and rude with friends. It's truly so hard to tame our tongues. But if praise to God is always in our mouths like Psalm 34 says, then there won't be much room for negativity, right? Another scripture says, "You must pray at all times as the Holy Spirit leads you to pray. Pray for the things that are needed. You must watch and keep on praying" (Ephesians 6:18 NLV). When we do our best to think of these two scriptures, our minds and tongues will be busy doing good things instead of maybe getting us into trouble!

• •

Heavenly Father, I want my mind and mouth to be full of prayer and praise continually. Please help me to keep my focus on You! Amen.

YOU HAVE MARTHA AND MARY'S EXAMPLE

A woman named Martha welcomed him into her house. And she had a sister called Mary, who sat at the Lord's feet and listened to his teaching.
LUKE 10:38–39 ESV

Two sisters named Mary and Martha were excited to welcome Jesus into their home. Martha was very good at hosting and knew all the details of planning and preparing. Since Jesus was such an honored guest, she probably wanted everything to be perfect. But Martha grew very frustrated with Mary because when Jesus arrived, Mary didn't help her with all the work of hosting and serving. Mary simply sat at Jesus' feet to listen to everything He had to say. Both sisters loved Jesus and were showing it in their own ways. But Jesus lovingly told Martha that Mary had chosen what was best, not fussing much over the details of hosting Him but simply enjoying His company and listening to His teaching.

* *

Dear Jesus, I want to show my love for You in the details, like Martha, but I also want to choose the best way by enjoying simply being with You, like Mary. Help me to balance these things well. Amen.

SOMEDAY ALL THINGS WILL BE NEW

Then I saw "a new heaven and a new earth," for the first heaven and the first earth had passed away, and there was no longer any sea.... And I heard a loud voice from the throne saying, "Look! God's dwelling place is now among the people, and he will dwell with them. They will be his people, and God himself will be with them and be their God. 'He will wipe every tear from their eyes. There will be no more death' or mourning or crying or pain, for the old order of things has passed away."

REVELATION 21:1, 3–4 NIV

Maybe our minds could never fully understand how awesome it will be (see 1 Corinthians 2:9)—maybe that's why the Bible doesn't give us a whole lot of specific detail about what forever life will be like. But it does tell us everything will be new and there will be no more death or sorrow or crying or pain. That fact alone shows us how truly awesome and wonderful our new life will be!

• •

Heavenly Father, I can't even imagine how amazing life will be when You make Your home with us in the new heaven and earth You have planned. Until then, please keep me close to You, through Your Word and through prayer, as I do the good things You have for me in this life. Thank You! Amen.

YOU WILL NEVER BE ABANDONED OR DESTROYED

*We are hard pressed on every side, but not crushed;
perplexed, but not in despair; persecuted, but not
abandoned; struck down, but not destroyed.*

2 CORINTHIANS 4:8–9 NIV

We've all had days when every single thing seems to be going wrong. Maybe we even have weeks or months like that, times when we feel so discouraged we wonder when God is ever going to step in to rescue us or at least protect us from any more trouble. This scripture promises that no matter how discouraged we feel, God will never let us get to a point where we cannot handle our discouragement. Sometimes He will wait until the last moment, but He will always provide a way out. He lets us experience hard things at times to teach us new lessons and show us how strong we can be in all kinds of situations when we depend on Him.

* *

*Heavenly Father, please help me to keep hanging in there when
I feel discouraged and confused and in pain. I know You never
abandon me, and You have good plans and blessings for me. Amen.*

BLESSED BY UNITY

*Be patient with each other, making allowance for each other's
faults because of your love. Make every effort to keep yourselves
united in the Spirit, binding yourselves together with peace.*
EPHESIANS 4:2–3 NLT

The Bible talks a lot about how Christians should have good relationships and unity. Being like-minded and standing strong together, mutually encouraged by our common love of our Savior, Jesus Christ, is a real blessing. Jesus even prayed this for all believers: "I am praying not only for these disciples but also for all who will ever believe in me through their message. I pray that they will all be one, just as you and I are one—as you are in me, Father, and I am in you. And may they be in us so that the world will believe you sent me. I have given them the glory you gave me, so they may be one as we are one. I am in them and you are in me. May they experience such perfect unity that the world will know that you sent me and that you love them as much as you love me" (John 17:20–23 NLT).

• •

*Dear Jesus, please help me to do my part to encourage and maintain
unity with others I know who love and follow You too. Amen.*

LOOK AT THE NIGHT SKY

The holy God asks, "Who compares with me? Is anyone my equal?" Look at the evening sky! Who created the stars? Who gave them each a name? Who leads them like an army? The LORD is so powerful that none of the stars are ever missing.

ISAIAH 40:25–26 CEV

Think about this scripture when you look up at the night sky. When you consider how vast the sky is and how God is so much bigger that He actually has a name for each star, you'll be blown away! We can't help but be filled with awe and gratitude and confidence when we trust that the same great big God who made the heavens and knows the stars by name made us and knows our names and takes good care of us too. Our blessings truly are out-of-this-world amazing!

• •

Almighty God, I can't even wrap my mind around how awesome You are and how blessed I am to be Yours! Thank You that I can talk to You about anything and depend on You for everything! Amen.

DON'T FORGET

Let all that I am praise the LORD; with my whole heart, I will praise his holy name. Let all that I am praise the LORD; may I never forget the good things he does for me. He forgives all my sins and heals all my diseases. He redeems me from death and crowns me with love and tender mercies.

PSALM 103:1–4 NLT

We unfortunately get forgetful sometimes. Especially as a teen in school, you have so many things to keep track of and remember, and some things slip your mind. But let this psalm encourage you to never forget the many ways God blesses you. If you're ever feeling discouraged while you wait and hope and pray for a new blessing, stop to think about all that God has already given you and provided for you—especially your salvation and new life in Him. He loves you and has never failed you in the past. He will not fail you now or in the future.

* *

Heavenly Father, forgive me when I forget all that You do for me and the zillions of ways You have already blessed me. I see Your hand and Your love and Your care in my life in the past and in the present, and I trust You to provide for me in the future. Amen.

GOD'S LOVE FOR YOU IS UNSTOPPABLE

If God is for us, who can ever be against us?
ROMANS 8:31 NLT

You might feel intimidated by or even afraid of certain people sometimes, but if you stop to remember who is living in you and working through you—the Holy Spirit of the one and only Creator God Himself!—then truly no one is powerful enough to be against you. No one is greater than Almighty God who loves you so much that He sent His Son to die to save you. Romans 8:38–39 (NLV) goes on to reassure: "Nothing can keep us from the love of God. Death cannot! Life cannot! Angels cannot! Leaders cannot! Any other power cannot! Hard things now or in the future cannot! The world above or the world below cannot! Any other living thing cannot keep us away from the love of God which is ours through Christ Jesus our Lord."

Almighty God, no one else is like You, and I'm so blessed and grateful to be Your child. Absolutely nothing can keep Your great love away from me, and that assurance fills me with joy and hope and confidence. Thank You! Amen.

YOU HAVE FOREVER BLESSINGS

"Do not lay up for yourselves treasures on earth, where moth and rust destroy and where thieves break in and steal, but lay up for yourselves treasures in heaven, where neither moth nor rust destroys and where thieves do not break in and steal. For where your treasure is, there your heart will be also."
MATTHEW 6:19–21 ESV

The things you have in this world are nice, for sure. It's fun to collect things and get new clothes and jewelry and technology and stuff for your room and entertainment and vacations and all kinds of gifts and blessings, right? And it's okay to enjoy those things—as long as we don't fixate on them and worship them, making getting all that stuff our main motivation and goal. Nothing here on this earth lasts forever. Things break or wear out or get lost. Entertainment and vacations come to an end. You can't take one bit of your stuff on to heaven with you when your life on earth is over. So God tells us to store up treasures in heaven. That's where our blessings last forever. How do we do that? We ask God to show us the good works He has planned for us to do, and we love and follow and obey Him. We constantly make it our goal to live out what Jesus said are the two greatest commandments—to love God with all our heart, soul, mind, and strength, and to love others like we love ourselves (Matthew 22:36–40).

Heavenly Father, help me to focus on the forever treasures that await me in heaven. Amen.

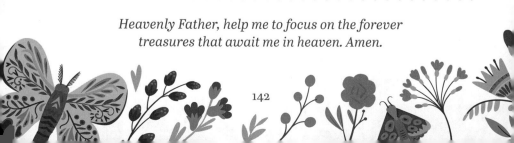

YOU KNOW THE WAY

"Don't let your hearts be troubled. Trust in God, and trust also in me. There is more than enough room in my Father's home. If this were not so, would I have told you that I am going to prepare a place for you? When everything is ready, I will come and get you, so that you will always be with me where I am. And you know the way to where I am going." "No, we don't know, Lord," Thomas said. "We have no idea where you are going, so how can we know the way?" Jesus told him, "I am the way, the truth, and the life. No one can come to the Father except through me."

JOHN 14:1–7 NLT

Thomas wanted details, maybe even a map, to know exactly how to get to the home Jesus promised He was getting ready. But Jesus said *He* is the way, truth, and life, and no one comes to God except through Him. In other words, Jesus is the map to follow to heaven. We follow Him by reading His Word and doing our best to live like Him, always trusting that He alone saved us from sin when He died on the cross. And because He rose to life again, we know we will too!

• •

Dear Jesus, nothing means more to me than knowing You as my Savior. Thank You for being our map to heaven! I trust You are the one and only way, truth, and life. Amen.

YOU CAN PRAY TO GOD MORNING, NOON, AND NIGHT

I ask for your help, Lord God, and you will keep me safe. Morning, noon, and night you hear my concerns and my complaints. I am attacked from all sides, but you will rescue me unharmed by the battle. You have always ruled, and you will hear me.

PSALM 55:16–19 CEV

It's good to have a set daily quiet time with God to read the Bible and pray. But we shouldn't let that be the only time we talk with God throughout the day. This psalm reminds us that morning, noon, and night, God hears each one of our prayers. He's ready to listen every moment in between too as well as all night long. If you wake up from a nightmare or a storm or a strange noise, the very first thing you can do is cry out to God in prayer for help and comfort! What a blessing! Isn't it amazing that every single person in the world can pray this way at any time too? We have an awesome heavenly Father!

• •

Father God, thank You for being available every moment of every day to hear from me! Amen.

YOU HAVE A SAFE PLACE FOREVER

My soul is quiet and waits for God alone. My hope comes from Him.
He alone is my rock and the One Who saves me. He is my strong place.
I will not be shaken. My being safe and my honor rest with God. My
safe place is in God, the rock of my strength. Trust in Him at all times,
O people. Pour out your heart before Him. God is a safe place for us.

Psalm 62:5–8 NLV

When you think of your safe place, do you think of the place you feel most comfortable and relaxed and understood? Maybe you think of being at home with your family, cozy and well taken care of. Or maybe you think of your safe place as with your best friend, the one you can talk to about anything. Those are good safe places, but they're not eternal like God is. He wants to be your best, rock-solid, forever safe place! He is with you anytime and anywhere. Talk to Him, cry out to Him, depend on Him, and trust Him for everything you need.

* *

Heavenly Father, I'm so blessed that You are my unchanging, eternal
safe place. Thank You that I can pour out my heart to You and be
loved and understood—anytime, anywhere, forever. Amen.

YOU CAN PRAY ALL THE TIME, ABOUT EVERYTHING

*Don't worry about anything; instead, pray about everything.
Tell God what you need, and thank him for all he has done.
Then you will experience God's peace, which exceeds
anything we can understand. His peace will guard your
hearts and minds as you live in Christ Jesus.*

PHILIPPIANS 4:6–7 NLT

What a crazy cool blessing that the almighty, one true God of the universe wants you to talk to Him all the time. His Word tells us again and again to keep on praying to Him for everything, at all times. It literally says, "Never stop praying" (1 Thessalonians 5:17 NLT). Prayer is never just talking to yourself or to some fake god who doesn't care. Prayer is a direct line of communication with the King of all kings and Lord of all lords! Wow! He loves you enough that He sent His only Son, Jesus, to die to save you. He wants to empower you with courage and faith and joy in Him for whatever you're facing!

. . . .

Almighty God, my heavenly Father, I'm so grateful You want me to pray to You and never stop for any reason. Thank You that You are always with me, always listening to me. I love You, Lord! Amen.

THE HEART OF A LION

The sinful run away when no one is trying to catch them, but those who are right with God have as much strength of heart as a lion.
PROVERBS 28:1 NLV

If you are right with God, meaning you have confessed your sin and asked Jesus to be your Savior, this scripture tells you that you are as bold and brave as a lion. That's a great blessing, especially in this crazy world. People who don't trust Jesus as Savior are often so afraid of every little thing that they're running even when there is no danger. They might never admit that, but deep down they have no faith to give them courage. But everyone who trusts Jesus as Savior does have faith. We are right with God because of Jesus, and so we are able to be as courageous as the mightiest lion.

* *

Dear Jesus, I trust You, and I know You make me right with God. I have nothing to fear. I am blessed to be courageous and strong because of You! Amen.

YOU HAVE HOPE THAT OVERPOWERS GRIEF

Dear brothers and sisters, we want you to know what will happen to the believers who have died so you will not grieve like people who have no hope. For since we believe that Jesus died and was raised to life again, we also believe that when Jesus returns, God will bring back with him the believers who have died.

1 THESSALONIANS 4:13–14 NLT

Maybe you've experienced the loss of a family member or friend. The pain and sadness are excruciating. But even while you cry, even while you desperately miss them, you can have hope that overpowers the pain and sadness—because if your loved one trusted Jesus, then he or she will be brought to life again just as Jesus rose to life again. That is an extraordinary comfort—and it should motivate us to share the good news of Jesus with those around us. Just like God does, we should want all people to be saved from sin (see 1 Timothy 2:4).

• •

Heavenly Father, I'm so very grateful for the overpowering hope You give us because of Jesus. Help me to share the good news, and help others to put their trust in You so we all can be raised to life again and live with You forever. Amen.

YOUR GOD CAN RESCUE LIKE NO ONE ELSE CAN

"Shadrach, Meshach, and Abednego. . .pay no attention to you, Your Majesty. They refuse to serve your gods and do not worship the gold statue you have set up."
DANIEL 3:12 NLT

Three friends named Shadrach, Meshach, and Abednego loved God and refused to bow down to worship the false god the king had set up. They said, "If we are thrown into the blazing furnace, the God whom we serve is able to save us. He will rescue us from your power, Your Majesty. But even if he doesn't, we want to make it clear to you. . .that we will never serve your gods or worship the gold statue you have set up" (Daniel 3:17–18 NLT). So they were thrown into a fire that should have killed them instantly. Instead, they walked around in that furnace and not even one hair on their heads was burnt. In fact, they even had some company join them in the fire—an angel of God! When the king let them out, he praised the one true God and ordered that no one could speak against Him. He said, "There is no other god who can rescue like this!" (Daniel 3:29 NLT).

Heavenly Father, thank You for the example of Shadrach, Meshach, and Abednego. I want to be as faithful and brave as they were and never bow to anyone but You, no matter what! I believe no one is able to rescue like You can! Amen.

YOUR PATHS WILL BE STRAIGHT

Do not forget my teaching, but keep my commands in your heart, for they will prolong your life many years and bring you peace and prosperity. . . . Trust in the LORD with all your heart and lean not on your own understanding; in all your ways submit to him, and he will make your paths straight.

PROVERBS 3:1–2, 5–6 NIV

Even though so many movies and messages and people today will tell you to "follow your heart," that's not actually great advice. Before any of us really do follow our heart, we need to make sure our heart matches up with God's. Too often our own hearts and desires are tempted by sin and everything that's bad for us. So God's Word tells us to trust Him with all our hearts and to *not* lean on our own understanding. We need to stay close to Him by reading His Word, praying, worshipping Him, and serving Him. And we need to ask Him every day to help us submit to Him and His will for us—that's the only way we stay on a good, straight path.

Father God, I want to trust in You more than myself. Please help me to follow my own heart only when it's matching up with Yours because I'm submitted to You and Your will. Amen.

YOU HAVE SOMEONE TO LIFT YOUR HEAD

You, O Lord, are a covering around me, my shining-greatness, and the One Who lifts my head. I was crying to the Lord with my voice. And He answered me from His holy mountain. I lay down and slept, and I woke up again, for the Lord keeps me safe.

PSALM 3:3–5 NLV

Sometimes you just need to go to your bed and cry your eyes out. And that's okay! Life can be crazy, and sometimes everything feels way too hard. As you cry and release all that emotion, think of God as being like your favorite blanket comforting you, just as this scripture says He is the covering around you. He is the one who helps you and gives you "shining-greatness" again. He lifts your head and wants to help you get out of bed and face all the hard things head-on with His power. It's good to cry to God and tell Him all your feelings, but then be sure to let Him lift your head and empower you to keep on going.

* *

Heavenly Father, I'm so grateful You comfort and cover me when I'm crying to You. And then You lift my head again. I can face anything with You as my constant encouragement and strength. Amen.

YOU HAVE THE BEST NEWS TO SHARE

I am not ashamed of the Good News. It is the power of God. It is the way He saves men from the punishment of their sins if they put their trust in Him. It is for the Jew first and for all other people also. The Good News tells us we are made right with God by faith in Him. Then, by faith we live that new life through Him.

ROMANS 1:16–17 NLV

No matter how the world around us loves to make fun of Christians, we should never feel embarrassed or ashamed of the gospel message—the good news of Jesus Christ. Like the apostle Paul in the Bible, we should all want to be able to say this: we are not ashamed of the message that Jesus came to earth to live a perfect life and teach us, then died on the cross to pay for our sins, and then rose to life again and now offers us eternal life too. When we share this good news with others, we help spread God's power to save people from their sins.

• •

Heavenly Father, please forgive me for ever feeling ashamed to share the good news about Jesus! I want to be bold and generous in sharing the gospel, no matter what people think. Thank You for wanting to save all people from their sins! Amen.

YOU CAN FOCUS ON ALL
GOD IS ABLE TO DO

*"Praise the name of God forever and ever, for he has all wisdom
and power. He controls the course of world events; he removes
kings and sets up other kings. He gives wisdom to the wise and
knowledge to the scholars. He reveals deep and mysterious
things and knows what lies hidden in darkness, though he
is surrounded by light. I thank and praise you, God of my
ancestors, for you have given me wisdom and strength."*
DANIEL 2:20–23 NLT

Daniel in the lions' den isn't just a cool Sunday school story. It's a true
account of great faith and prayer and obedience and courage that we all
need to read and remember again and again. This scripture from Daniel
2 is part of Daniel's prayer to God, worshipping Him for all the amazing
things He is able to do. You will be blessed when you let it encourage
and strengthen you too.

⸱ ⸱

*Heavenly Father, like Daniel, I always want to remember everything
You are able to do. I want to worship You and take courage as I
focus on Your power and works—past, present, and future. Amen.*

YOUR SADNESS CAN TURN TO JOY

"Hear me, LORD, and have mercy on me. Help me, O LORD." You have turned my mourning into joyful dancing. You have taken away my clothes of mourning and clothed me with joy, that I might sing praises to you and not be silent. O LORD my God, I will give you thanks forever!
PSALM 30:10–12 NLT

Only the one true God can take the worst kind of sadness or anger or pain in our lives and turn it into such joy that we feel like dancing. He might do that for us here on earth in certain ways, or we might have to wait until heaven, but He promises that He will. With every hard and sad thing you go through, you have a choice either to let your circumstances make you angry with God and pull you apart from Him or to trust His promises and grow closer to Him. The first choice will only make you sadder and sadder, but the second choice will make you do some happy dancing!

· ·

Heavenly Father, please keep me close to You and strong in my faith in the midst of every kind of pain. I trust that in Your perfect timing, You will turn all heartache and struggle into total joy. Amen.

EVEN WHILE YOU'RE YOUNG

Don't let anyone think less of you because you are young.
Be an example to all believers in what you say, in the way
you live, in your love, your faith, and your purity.
1 TIMOTHY 4:12 NLT

Even while you're young, you can be an example to others showing how
blessed you are to know Jesus Christ as your Savior and to live for Him.
Let them see how it's the best kind of life. You can learn God's Word and
follow it. You can choose to love God and others well and treat everyone
with respect and kindness. You can work hard at everything you do as
a way to bring praise to God, not yourself. You won't do all these things
perfectly, and that's okay. But you can try your best and know that as a
young person living your life devoted to God, you are setting an excellent
example for others to follow!

Heavenly Father, please help me even while I'm young to set a
great example of how to love and live for You! I'm so very blessed
by You, and I want others to be blessed by You too! Amen.

ENCOURAGEMENT AND FELLOWSHIP

Let us hold tightly without wavering to the hope we affirm, for God can be trusted to keep his promise. Let us think of ways to motivate one another to acts of love and good works. And let us not neglect our meeting together, as some people do, but encourage one another, especially now that the day of his return is drawing near.
HEBREWS 10:23–25 NLT

What is your church like? How involved are you? It matters so much that you are connected to a solid Bible-teaching church where you can enjoy the blessings God wants to give you by way of gathering with other believers. When we meet together to worship God and learn more from His Word, we gain such great encouragement to stay strong in our faith and never let go of our hope in Jesus and all of God's promises. When we meet together, we help to keep shining God's light in a dark world where so many more people need to find their way to salvation in Jesus Christ. And when we meet together, we enjoy fellowship with one another and serve one another. We can share our struggles and needs and joys with each other and help each other carry the heavy burdens and stresses of this life.

Father God, all of my life, please help me to make it a priority to be active in a solid Bible-teaching church that is obedient and honoring to You. Thank You for the great blessings of encouragement and fellowship with other believers! Amen.

GOD HELPS YOU FROM THE HIGHEST HEAVENS

Our holy God lives forever in the highest heavens, and this is what he says: Though I live high above in the holy place, I am here to help those who are humble and depend only on me.

ISAIAH 57:15 CEV

Imagine if you could pick up the phone and call the president of the United States and ask him for help with anything at any time. The role of president is a powerful one, so you would feel confident knowing that the president could come to your rescue for anything you asked. Even though not many of us are going to have close connections with important world leaders, the fact is we do have a close connection to the highest King and ultimate world ruler—our one true God who lives in the highest heavens! We have instant communication with Him through the Holy Spirit living within us, and He promises to help everyone who is humble and depends on Him above all. What an amazing blessing!

* *

Almighty God, You are the highest and best and most powerful of all, and yet You love me and want to help me. I am amazed and thankful, and I love You too! Amen.

FREED FROM FEAR

I will praise the LORD at all times. I will constantly speak his praises. I will boast only in the LORD; let all who are helpless take heart. Come, let us tell of the LORD's greatness; let us exalt his name together. I prayed to the LORD, and he answered me. He freed me from all my fears. Those who look to him for help will be radiant with joy; no shadow of shame will darken their faces. In my desperation I prayed, and the LORD listened; he saved me from all my troubles. For the angel of the LORD is a guard; he surrounds and defends all who fear him.

PSALM 34:1–7 NLT

People who have been in bad car accidents are likely to struggle with a fear of driving. People who have been bitten by dogs are likely to have a fear of dogs. People who have had close calls with tornadoes or hurricanes are likely to be nervous whenever bad weather hits. No doubt, our scary experiences affect us. But God knows each of us individually. He knows all about every hard thing we've ever been through. He knows every detail about us, even the exact number of hairs on our heads (Luke 12:7)! So we can admit every bit of fear and anxiety and let Him take those feelings from us and fill us instead with His peace!

* *

Heavenly Father, You know exactly the reasons I struggle with certain kinds of fear and anxiety. Please encourage me in the specific ways I need in order to overcome those fears and thrive. Amen.

BLESSED BY YOUR GO-TO GROUP

*Therefore, confess your sins to one another and pray
for one another, that you may be healed. The prayer of a
righteous person has great power as it is working.*

JAMES 5:16 ESV

Think of the people in your life whom you can talk to about absolutely anything—the family and friends you can trust the most. You are blessed to have them as your go-to group, so thank them and thank God for them. With them on your side, no matter what you're facing, you know you have a support system. You can share your problems, fears, worries, and praises with your go-to group. You can confess any sins and pray together. Each prayer with a loved one is a boost to your confidence and courage, a blessing from God as He hears each prayer and reaches out to help. Thank God for your group, and also ask Him to show You how you should share the love and blessings of your group, reaching out to include and encourage even more people.

* *

*Heavenly Father, thank You for family and friends who love
You first and who love me, support me, and pray for me. Please
always put these kinds of people in my life, and help me to be
faithful to love, support, and pray for them too. Amen.*

YOU HAVE ANCESTORS TO LOOK UP TO

Faith makes us sure of what we hope for and gives us proof of what we cannot see. It was their faith that made our ancestors pleasing to God. Because of our faith, we know that the world was made at God's command. We also know that what can be seen was made out of what cannot be seen.
HEBREWS 11:1–3 CEV

Do you *always* have faith to believe that God will do what He has promised? Probably not always because sometimes our faith slips a bit. So anytime you feel like your faith is weak or you're losing your grip on it, Hebrews 11 is a great chapter to read to strengthen your faith again. It will remind you of many Bible heroes who continued to believe that God would do what He promised even when it seemed impossible. Whatever you are needing God to do that might seem totally crazy, keep trusting Him today and every day.

• •

Heavenly Father, I want to be like the many faith heroes in the Bible who kept believing in You even when life was confusing and hard. Amen.

GOD CAN SPEAK TO YOU IN AMAZING WAYS

*There the angel of the L*ORD *appeared to him in a blazing fire from the middle of a bush. Moses stared in amazement. Though the bush was engulfed in flames, it didn't burn up. "This is amazing," Moses said to himself. "Why isn't that bush burning up? I must go see it." When the L*ORD *saw Moses coming to take a closer look, God called to him from the middle of the bush, "Moses! Moses!"*

EXODUS 3:2–4 NLT

God can speak to you through anything, in any kind of situation—like the amazing way He spoke to Moses through a burning bush. No one can know exactly why God chooses certain incredible ways to speak to His people, but it's just amazing to know He can! Listen to Him first and regularly through reading all of His Word, and also ask Him to speak to you in any kind of way He chooses. Let your heart and mind be open to hearing His voice!

Dear Lord, thank You for Your Word and the amazing ways You speak to Your people. Please speak to me and help me always to listen well. Amen.

YOU CAN WORSHIP NO MATTER WHAT

Around midnight Paul and Silas were praying and singing hymns to God, and the other prisoners were listening.
ACTS 16:25 NLT

On one of the apostle Paul's many travels, he and his friend Silas were put in jail. But this change of circumstances didn't hinder their faith. In fact, they used their jail time to worship God. Late at night while they were praying and singing and other prisoners were listening, suddenly an earthquake shook the jail. It was so strong that the prison doors flew open and everyone's chains broke loose! The jailer woke up and was terrified. He thought he would be killed if all the prisoners escaped. But Paul said to him, "We are all here!" And the jailer ran to Paul and Silas and brought them out of their jail cell and said, "What must I do to be saved?"

They told him, "Believe in the Lord Jesus and you will be saved, along with everyone in your household" (Acts 16: 31 NLT). Then the jailer took Paul and Silas to his home and fed them a meal. And everyone in his family listened to Paul and Silas and believed in Jesus.

Heavenly Father, even in the worst situations, help me to keep on worshipping You just like Paul and Silas did. They were so blessed to experience a great miracle and to help others know You as Savior too! Amen.

YOU ARE GIFTED

Each of you has been blessed with one of God's many wonderful gifts to be used in the service of others. So use your gift well. If you have the gift of speaking, preach God's message. If you have the gift of helping others, do it with the strength that God supplies. Everything should be done in a way that will bring honor to God because of Jesus Christ, who is glorious and powerful forever. Amen.

1 PETER 4:10–11 CEV

The talents and things you're naturally good at and that come easy to you are the gifts God has given you. He has given them to you so you can help others with them. If you're good at certain school subjects, see what you can do to help your friends who struggle with them. If you're especially friendly and outgoing, reach out to people to make them feel included. If you have talents in music, see how you can use them to help worship God at church. Most of all, continually thank God and give Him credit for every good thing you can do. Each one is a gift from Him!

Heavenly Father, thank You for the unique talents and abilities You've given me. I want to use all of them to worship You and point others to You. Amen.

YOU CAN STAY IN SHAPE

Have nothing to do with godless myths and old wives' tales; rather, train yourself to be godly. For physical training is of some value, but godliness has value for all things, holding promise for both the present life and the life to come. This is a trustworthy saying that deserves full acceptance. That is why we labor and strive, because we have put our hope in the living God, who is the Savior of all people, and especially of those who believe.

1 TIMOTHY 4:7–10 NIV

There are seemingly endless popular ways to keep your body in shape these days. And that's good. The Bible tells us we definitely should take good care of our bodies (see 1 Corinthians 6:19–20). But even more important, the Bible tells us we should grow in godliness. We should strive to learn more and more about God and to live like His Son, Jesus. Physical fitness here on earth matters for a little while, but growing strong in knowing and loving God matters for forever.

* *

Heavenly Father, I want to be in the right kind of shape. Please help me to be physically fit but more importantly to be spiritually fit by growing closer and closer to You. Amen.

TRULY NO WORRIES

"Do not worry about your life, what you will eat or drink; or about your body, what you will wear. Is not life more than food, and the body more than clothes? Look at the birds of the air; they do not sow or reap or store away in barns, and yet your heavenly Father feeds them. Are you not much more valuable than they? Can any one of you by worrying add a single hour to your life? And why do you worry about clothes? See how the flowers of the field grow. They do not labor or spin. Yet I tell you that not even Solomon in all his splendor was dressed like one of these. . . . But seek first his kingdom and his righteousness, and all these things will be given to you as well. Therefore do not worry about tomorrow, for tomorrow will worry about itself. Each day has enough trouble of its own."

MATTHEW 6:25–29, 33–34 NIV

"No worries" is a nice thing to say, but the only one who can truly bless us with no worries is our good heavenly Father who cares the very most about us, even more than our closest friends and loved ones. If He knows and takes good care of even the birds and the flowers that He created, surely He takes even better care of the people He made in His own image.

· ·

Father God, thank You for the blessing of truly no worries when I focus on Your great big love and Your all-knowing care for me. Amen.

IN THE MIDST OF SUFFERING AND MISUNDERSTANDING

What we are suffering now cannot compare with the glory that will be shown to us.
ROMANS 8:18 CEV

Sometimes when we're struggling with a problem or need or heart-ache, God doesn't just suddenly fix things like we hope. We sure wish He would, and we pray and cry out to Him, asking Him to see our needs and make everything okay again right away. And when He doesn't, our trust in Him can really be shaken as we wonder why. We question God. Maybe we even feel anger and blame toward Him at times—but anger and blame are not good to hold on to. Even when we're confused and hurting and frustrated over a prayer that seems to go unanswered, we need to look for the ways God is answering other prayers and showing His love in many other ways at the same time. We can continue to trust and know that we're blessed even through the hardest times. We can't possibly see all the good things God is doing in the midst of suffering, but one day in heaven we will understand. Then God will make all things perfect and new.

* *

Dear Lord, please help me to keep trusting You even when I'm confused about what You're doing. When I don't see You answering my prayers as I want them to be answered, please show me and remind me of how You are caring for me and blessing me in other ways. Amen.

YOU HAVE REAL JOY

"As the Father has loved me, so have I loved you. Now remain in my love. If you keep my commands, you will remain in my love, just as I have kept my Father's commands and remain in his love. I have told you this so that my joy may be in you and that your joy may be complete. My command is this: Love each other as I have loved you. Greater love has no one than this: to lay down one's life for one's friends."

JOHN 15:9–13 NIV

The world around you tries to sell you all kinds of ideas about what love and joy are, and often they're really bad ideas. But Jesus tells you here in John 15 how to have *real* love and joy. When we obey Jesus the way Jesus obeyed God the Father, we stay close to God. And because God is love (see 1 John 4:8), our whole lives are lived in love. When we live in love, we can't help but be full of joy because we are living exactly the way God intended when He created us!

Dear Jesus, I'm sorry for the times I don't obey You. Every time I disobey, I want to realize my mistake and come back to You to get on the right track again. I want to live in Your love and be full of real joy! Amen.

YOU HAVE GOD GUIDING YOU

By day the LORD went ahead of them in a pillar of cloud to guide them on their way and by night in a pillar of fire to give them light, so that they could travel by day or night. Neither the pillar of cloud by day nor the pillar of fire by night left its place in front of the people.

EXODUS 13:21–22 NIV

God is the very best guide. When He led His people, the Israelites, out of slavery in Egypt, He did so with a pillar of cloud during the day and a pillar of fire at night to give them light. That must have been unbelievably cool to see! When you read this story in the Bible, remember that God wants to be your guide. No, He may not lead you in such dramatic ways as pillars of cloud and fire, but you can ask Him to show you clearly step-by-step, day by day, the places He wants you to go and the good things He wants you to do. And make sure you're spending time learning from His Word, especially because it's a lamp to your feet and a light for your path (Psalm 119:105).

. . . .

Heavenly Father, I want You to be my guide. I trust that You can use anything to lead me in my life. Please help me to keep my attention focused on You. Show me all the good places and plans You have for me. Thank You! Amen.

THE ONE WHO LIVES IN YOU

The One Who lives in you is stronger than the one who is in the world.
1 JOHN 4:4 NLV

This is such a simple and powerful Bible verse to memorize and keep on repeat in your mind. Our enemy Satan is constantly stirring up all kinds of evil in this world. And you will be under attack from him sometimes in all sorts of different ways—through someone else's nasty words or actions, through stressful times for your family, through painful times of loss, through sickness, and on and on. But no matter how strong the enemy and his evil may seem against you and your loved ones, they are never stronger than the power of God in you through the Holy Spirit. Don't ever forget that! Call on God to help you be strong and calm and patient—and to help you see how He is working and taking care of you through it all.

* *

Father God, deep down I know You are always stronger than any attack on me, any hard thing I'm going through. But I do forget that truth sometimes, and I'm sorry. Please remind me and fill me with Your power and peace—and do the fighting for me. Amen.

REMEMBER THE POWER OF YOUR TONGUE

We all stumble in many ways. Anyone who is never at fault in what they say is perfect, able to keep their whole body in check. When we put bits into the mouths of horses to make them obey us, we can turn the whole animal. Or take ships as an example. Although they are so large and are driven by strong winds, they are steered by a very small rudder wherever the pilot wants to go. Likewise, the tongue is a small part of the body, but it makes great boasts. Consider what a great forest is set on fire by a small spark. . . . With the tongue we praise our Lord and Father, and with it we curse human beings, who have been made in God's likeness. Out of the same mouth come praise and cursing. My brothers and sisters, this should not be.

JAMES 3:2–5, 9–10 NIV

God's Word is crystal clear in James 3: we can bless and be blessed with the power of our tongue, or we can cause much damage and pain to others and ourselves with the power of our tongue. Every day (maybe even every minute in stressful situations!) we should ask God to help us exercise self-control and choose our words carefully.

· ·

Heavenly Father, thank You for understanding what a challenge it is to control my tongue. I ask You for Your help to use the power of my words well—to be a blessing to others and be blessed myself in return. Amen.

YOUR GOD NEVER CHANGES

"Long ago you laid the foundation of the earth and made the heavens with your hands. They will perish, but you remain forever; they will wear out like old clothing. You will change them like a garment and discard them. But you are always the same; you will live forever. The children of your people will live in security. Their children's children will thrive in your presence."

PSALM 102:25–28 NLT

Life is always changing, and sometimes we appreciate that fact and sometimes we don't. What is something you wish could always stay the same? What is something that you're glad always changes? No matter what changes around us, though, it's so good to know that God is constantly the same. We sure need His stability in this turbulent world. We depend on Him to be steady and strong and true, and when we look to Him to guide us, we can be steady and strong and true too!

• •

Heavenly Father, I'm glad You never change, and I'm especially glad that Your love and care for me never change. Please keep helping and guiding me. Amen.

YOU CAN BE A MIGHTY WARRIOR

When the angel of the LORD appeared to Gideon,
he said, "The LORD is with you, mighty warrior."
JUDGES 6:12 NIV

Think of a person you really look up to. How does it make you feel when they give you a wonderful compliment? Pretty nice, right? So imagine how Gideon must have felt when God spoke to him through an angel's appearance and called him a "mighty warrior." Wow!

You can think of God telling you the same thing He told Gideon. You are totally capable of being a mighty warrior for God, because He is with you always, constantly giving you courage and power. Those qualities don't come from yourself but from God's Holy Spirit within you.

- -

Dear Lord, I trust that You are with me in everything
I do. I want to be a mighty warrior who points other
people to You and Your love and truth! Amen.

HUMBLE AND HOME AGAIN

"This younger son packed all his belongings and moved to a distant land, and there he wasted all his money in wild living."
LUKE 15:13 NLT

One of Jesus' parables in the Bible was about a father who divided all that he owned between his two sons. The younger son took all of his inheritance and went to another country far away. He spent everything he had on living a wild and crazy life. After all his money was gone, he was hungry and friendless, and the only job he could find was feeding pigs. Then he began to think about what he had done and was ashamed of himself. So he got up and started for home. While he was still a long way off, his father saw him and felt full of love and kindness toward him. He ran to his son and threw his arms around him. The son said, "Father, I have sinned against both heaven and you, and I am no longer worthy of being called your son" (Luke 15:19 nlt).

But the father said to his workmen, "Quick! Bring the finest robe in the house and put it on him. Get a ring for his finger and sandals for his feet. And kill the calf we have been fattening. We must celebrate with a feast, for this son of mine was dead and has now returned to life. He was lost, but now he is found" (Luke 15:21–24 nlt).

• •

Heavenly Father, please help me to realize when I've done wrong and be willing to be humble and return and repent to make things right. Thank You that You love me no matter what and want to bless me even after I've made mistakes. Amen.

YOU CAN PROVE AND SHARE YOUR FAITH

God gave us the courage to declare his Good News to you boldly, in spite of great opposition. So you can see we were not preaching with any deceit or impure motives or trickery. For we speak as messengers approved by God to be entrusted with the Good News. Our purpose is to please God, not people. He alone examines the motives of our hearts.

1 Thessalonians 2:2–4 NLT

When we suffer through hard things but still trust God and share the good news of Jesus, we help prove to others the truth that Jesus really is the one and only Savior and Son of God. We show others that He is worth believing in. God gives us the ability and courage to share the gospel boldly, no matter our situation. Just ask Him and trust Him and watch how He blesses! He knows your heart, and your goal should always be to please Him and not other people.

• •

Heavenly Father, I want to help others see the absolute truth of Your good news that Jesus is our one and only Savior. If I have to go through hard or challenging times to help prove that, please bless me with the strength and courage to do so. Amen.

YOU'RE AN OVERCOMER

Children, you belong to God, and you have defeated these enemies. God's Spirit is in you and is more powerful than the one who is in the world. These enemies belong to this world, and the world listens to them, because they speak its language. We belong to God.

1 JOHN 4:4–6 CEV

Have you ever heard someone brag that they're never afraid of anything? There is no way that's true. Everyone gets scared or anxious or worried about something some of the time. True bravery and courage come from admitting fears and worries and facing them anyway. So you can't be brave unless you first know that you were scared of something but chose to deal with it. And sometimes you deal with things so well that you totally overcome them—and then they're never a fear or worry again! With God's Holy Spirit working in you to help, you can face anything and overcome it. Jesus said, "I have told you these things, so that in me you may have peace. In this world you will have trouble. But take heart! I have overcome the world" (John 16:33 NIV).

• •

Heavenly Father, I admit my fears and worries and how much I need Your help with them. I believe with all my heart that You can help me overcome them. Amen.

175

YOU HAVE A RACE TO RUN

Therefore, since we are surrounded by such a great cloud of witnesses, let us throw off everything that hinders and the sin that so easily entangles. And let us run with perseverance the race marked out for us, fixing our eyes on Jesus, the pioneer and perfecter of faith. For the joy set before him he endured the cross, scorning its shame, and sat down at the right hand of the throne of God. Consider him who endured such opposition from sinners, so that you will not grow weary and lose heart.

HEBREWS 12:1–3 NIV

The Bible says God has a race marked out for you. He has planned the course of your life, and if you keep looking to Jesus, He will lead you on it. As you keep looking to Him, you also have to regularly get rid of anything in your life that tries to pull you away from following Him. So it's extremely important to keep reading the Bible and learning from others who love and follow Jesus—at church and in your family and friendships.

Dear Jesus, thank You for planning the course of my life, the race I should run. Please keep growing and strengthening my faith in You! Amen.

PEACE WILL KEEP YOUR HEART AND MIND

*The peace of God is much greater than the human
mind can understand. This peace will keep your
hearts and minds through Christ Jesus.*

PHILIPPIANS 4:7 NLV

Maybe schoolwork is extra hard these days, or maybe you just started a new semester or even a new school and everything feels different. Maybe you or a loved one is sick and needing a lot of medical care. Maybe there's a lot of conflict in your home or with your friend group. But no matter what is going on, God can give you extraordinary peace. If you focus on all the stress, of course you will be stressed. So focus instead on what Philippians 4 goes on to say: "Keep your minds thinking about whatever is true, whatever is respected, whatever is right, whatever is pure, whatever can be loved, and whatever is well thought of. If there is anything good and worth giving thanks for, think about these things. Keep on doing all the things you learned and received and heard from me. Do the things you saw me do. Then the God Who gives peace will be with you" (Philippians 4:8–9 NLV).

* *

*Father God, help me to trust You in the middle of stress and
stay focused on what is good and right and true. Please
bless me with Your extraordinary peace. Amen.*

ALMIGHTY GOD, KING OF ALL KINGS, LORD OF ALL LORDS

At just the right time Christ will be revealed from heaven by the blessed and only almighty God, the King of all kings and Lord of all lords. He alone can never die, and he lives in light so brilliant that no human can approach him. No human eye has ever seen him, nor ever will. All honor and power to him forever! Amen.

1 TIMOTHY 6:15–16 NLT

No one yet has ever fully seen God because He is so awesome that we humans just aren't able. It's a little like trying to look at the sun. We know the sun is there and we can see it and all the good it does, but our human eyes are unable to look at it directly because it's just too much! Our eyes were not made to look at something so bright. But someday, at just the right time, the Bible tells us, we will get to see God fully, and we will see how awesome and powerful He is over everything in all creation.

. . . .

Dear Lord, even now on earth while I can't fully see You, I trust that You are working in my life and guiding me. I'm so thankful that one day I will see You fully! I love You! Amen.

BETTER IS ONE DAY

*Better is one day in your courts than a thousand elsewhere; I would
rather be a doorkeeper in the house of my God than dwell in the tents
of the wicked. For the LORD God is a sun and shield; the LORD bestows
favor and honor; no good thing does he withhold from those whose
walk is blameless. LORD Almighty, blessed is the one who trusts in you.*
PSALM 84:10–12 NIV

Nothing you can do is better than loving and worshipping and obeying
the one true God. Nowhere you can go is better than being in His courts,
within His kingdom. No one is worthy of your worship like Him. No one
is able to protect and provide for you like Him. No one loves you like Him.
Girl, you are so indescribably blessed to be His child!

• •

*Almighty God, I praise You that I get to call You my
Father and Provider, my Friend and Savior through Jesus
Christ, My Comforter and Helper through the Holy Spirit.
One day with You is truly better than being anywhere else.
I'm so grateful that all of my days are with You! Amen.*

EVERY SPIRITUAL BLESSING

All praise to God, the Father of our Lord Jesus Christ, who has blessed us with every spiritual blessing in the heavenly realms because we are united with Christ. . . . So we praise God for the glorious grace he has poured out on us who belong to his dear Son. He is so rich in kindness and grace that he purchased our freedom with the blood of his Son and forgave our sins. He has showered his kindness on us, along with all wisdom and understanding.

God has now revealed to us his mysterious will regarding Christ—which is to fulfill his own good plan. And this is the plan: At the right time he will bring everything together under the authority of Christ—everything in heaven and on earth. Furthermore, because we are united with Christ, we have received an inheritance from God, for he chose us in advance, and he makes everything work out according to his plan.

EPHESIANS 1:3, 6–11 NLT

Wow! If ever you're in need of a huge dose of encouragement to remember just how blessed you are, girl, come again and again to Ephesians 1 and be filled with gratitude, joy, and praise that God gives you *every* spiritual blessing because you are united with Jesus Christ!

· ·

Father God, You're beyond amazing, and I love You! I can never thank You enough for every spiritual blessing You so generously give! Amen.

YOU CAN BE TOUGH IN THE TEASING AND THE TRIALS

Dear friends, don't be surprised at the fiery trials you are going through, as if something strange were happening to you. Instead, be very glad—for these trials make you partners with Christ in his suffering, so that you will have the wonderful joy of seeing his glory when it is revealed to all the world. If you are insulted because you bear the name of Christ, you will be blessed, for the glorious Spirit of God rests upon you. . . . If you are suffering in a manner that pleases God, keep on doing what is right, and trust your lives to the God who created you, for he will never fail you.

1 PETER 4:12–14, 19 NLT

If you are known for your faith in Jesus Christ as the one and only Savior, you will definitely be insulted and mocked in this world. Don't be surprised. You have to be tough in the midst of the insults and the teasing and the trials. But you never have to be tough on your own. Almighty God will never fail you.

* *

Father God, You have strength and power beyond anything I can imagine, and You give me strength and power to stand firm in my faith in You, no matter what kinds of trials I go through. I am strong and I am blessed—all because of You! Amen.

YOU HAVE POWER, LOVE, AND SELF-DISCIPLINE

The Spirit God gave us does not make us timid, but
gives us power, love and self-discipline.
2 TIMOTHY 1:7 NIV

This scripture passage is from the apostle Paul writing to his friend Timothy. He also told him, "I am reminded of your sincere faith, which first lived in your grandmother Lois and in your mother Eunice and, I am persuaded, now lives in you also" (2 Timothy 1:5 NIV). These words are for us to remember today too. May we always have sincere faith and look to those in our families and friend groups who inspire and encourage us to hold on tight to our faith. And may we also remember how blessed we are that the Holy Spirit within us never causes us to be afraid or ashamed or timid. No, the Spirit gives us power, love, and self-discipline. What specific ways are you needing to remember today that you have power, love, and self-discipline within you because of God's Holy Spirit?

• •

Heavenly Father, thank You so much for the gift of the
Holy Spirit and the strength and courage and abilities I
have because of Your presence within me, because of the
good work You are doing in and through me. Amen.

BLESSED BY YOUR GIVING, NO MATTER HOW SMALL

A poor widow came and dropped in two small coins.
MARK 12:42 NLT

One day Jesus watched as many rich people gave large offerings to God at the temple. Giving a lot wasn't hard for them to do because they were so rich that they had plenty of money to share. But then Jesus watched one woman, who was terribly poor and had no husband, drop in two coins worth less than one cent.

When Jesus saw this, He called out to His disciples, "This is the truth—this poor widow has given more money than all the others."

How could this be?

Jesus said, "The rich people put in money they didn't even need because they have so much extra. But the poor widow has nothing extra. She needed every bit of her money to live on, but still she gave it all to God."

. . . .

Dear Lord, help me to be faithful to You just like the widow in Jesus' story. She trusted You to provide for her no matter what, even when she gave until she had absolutely nothing left. I want to give to You in that same kind of way because I trust that Your blessings are greater than anything I could ever earn on my own. Amen.

JESUS WILL RETURN

The Spirit teaches you everything you need to know, and what he teaches is true—it is not a lie. So just as he has taught you, remain in fellowship with Christ. And now, dear children, remain in fellowship with Christ so that when he returns, you will be full of courage and not shrink back from him in shame.

1 JOHN 2:27–28 NLT

As Christians, we're supposed to be ready for Jesus to return to earth at any time (Matthew 24:44; Luke 12:40). To some people, that might sound ridiculous or scary, but for those of us who stay close to Jesus, it should be exciting and remind us how blessed we are! It should fill us with hope and joy! This scripture says that if we remain in fellowship with Jesus, meaning in close connection, then we will be full of courage and not shrink back with fear or be ashamed in any way when Jesus returns to earth.

* *

Dear Jesus, I believe You will return right on Your perfect schedule. Please keep me close to You. Help me to form good habits of spending time with You and to crave ever closer fellowship with You! Amen.

EVERYTHING REALLY WILL BE OKAY

We know that God makes all things work together for the good of those who love Him and are chosen to be a part of His plan. God knew from the beginning who would put their trust in Him. So He chose them and made them to be like His Son.

ROMANS 8:28–29 NLV

"Everything will be okay." We hear that a lot, and often we say it too. We need a lot of reassurance in this crazy, uncertain world. But sometimes things don't seem okay at all in the middle of hard situations and terrible circumstances. When major plans fall through, when we fail big-time, when a loved one dies, when our hearts are broken, and on and on—we don't feel like anything will be okay ever again! So we must trust in God's promise that says He is working all things together for the good of those who love Him and are part of His plans and purposes. Notice that the promise is not just for some things but for *all* things—even what seems like the absolute worst.

. . . .

Heavenly Father, please help me never to grow discouraged or hopeless, no matter how hard things get or how disappointed or heartbroken I may be. Keep me trusting in Your promise that You work all things together for good for those who love You. Amen.

THE GOOD THINGS OF HEAVEN

If then you have been raised with Christ, keep looking for the good things of heaven. This is where Christ is seated on the right side of God. Keep your minds thinking about things in heaven. . . . Christ is our life. When He comes again, you will also be with Him to share His shining-greatness.

COLOSSIANS 3:1–2, 4 NLV

Being raised with Christ means you are a Christian who believes in Jesus as your one and only Savior. It means you believe Jesus is God in human form, the Son whom Father God sent to live on earth and then die on the cross to take away your sin. Jesus did not stay dead but rose again. And when you believe in Him, you have been raised spiritually from the death that sin causes and you have the gift of forever life in heaven with Jesus. You are blessed by God, girl, and you get to keep looking ahead for the good things of heaven that are coming your way!

• •

Dear Jesus, I believe You are God and that You came to earth to teach us. Then You died to take away our sins and show us how much You love us. You rose again to life, and You make me rise to forever life because I trust in You as my one and only Savior. Thank You! Please help me to keep my mind always thinking about You and Your love. Amen.

SCRIPTURE INDEX

OLD TESTAMENT

NEW TESTAMENT